Reason and Mystery
in the Pentateuch

ביתו זו אשתו
לאה בת יוסף

Reason and Mystery in the Pentateuch

Aaron Streiter

WIPF & STOCK · Eugene, Oregon

REASON AND MYSTERY IN THE PENTATEUCH

Copyright © 2017 Aaron Streiter. All rights reserved. Except for brief quotations in critical publications or reviews, no part of this book may be reproduced in any manner without prior written permission from the publisher. Write: Permissions, Wipf and Stock Publishers, 199 W. 8th Ave., Suite 3, Eugene, OR 97401.

Wipf & Stock
An Imprint of Wipf and Stock Publishers
199 W. 8th Ave., Suite 3
Eugene, OR 97401

www.wipfandstock.com

PAPERBACK ISBN: 978-1-5326-1560-3
HARDCOVER ISBN: 978-1-5326-1562-7
EBOOK ISBN: 978-1-5326-1561-0

Manufactured in the U.S.A.   MARCH 23, 2017

The contributions to this study of Rabbi Mark Dratch, Professor Heinrich W. Guggenheimer, and Professor Steven T. Katz are gratefully acknowledged.

Reason and Mystery in the Pentateuch
AARON STREITER

The present study, addressed to traditionalist Jews concerned with theology, presents a fact, discusses the response it necessitates, and explains why a counter-response offered by some traditionalists is antithetical to traditionalism, and therefore without value to it.

The study defines traditionalist Jews concerned with theology as those Jews who believe that God revealed to the Jewish people, through Moses, at Mount Sinai, two works: the Pentateuch (the Written Law), revealed as a text, whose two major components are a sacred history, primarily of the Jewish people, and a codex, binding on the Jewish people; and the Mishnah (the Oral Law), an elucidation of the codex revealed orally, transmitted orally for generations, then redacted as a text; and that, as a result of divine decree and the diligence of Jewish traditionalists, the two works have been transmitted without corruption through some thirty-five hundred years, from the moment they were Revealed to the Jewish people at Mount Sinai to the present.[1] When the two works are considered together – as they must be, because they were revealed together, and are therefore equally sacred - they are called a single work, the Torah.

The belief is encapsulated in the following affirmation:

> This is the Torah that Moses presented before the Israelites (Deuteronomy 4:44), according to God's word through Moses (Numbers 9:23).[2]

---

1. See Appendix 1
2. *The Living Torah* [the Pentateuch], translated by Aryeh Kaplan. (New York: 1981). All quotations from the Pentateuch are taken from this volume.

The affirmation, recited whenever the scroll containing the Pentateuch is displayed during communal services, is taken as literal truth. Thus, to Jewish traditionalists it is axiomatic that some thirty-five hundred years ago, at Mount Sinai, God Revealed Himself to the Jews, and gave them the Torah, a work identical to the work they still study.

Moreover, they regard both the purpose and the value of the work as axiomatic. The purpose is to provide Jews, to whom God feels especially bound, a comprehensive guide to sacred history, and to conduct. And the work is uniquely valuable, because, as its Author alone is perfect, it alone is perfect.

That being the case, to traditionalist Jews it is in addition axiomatic that nothing can be more important than constant, exhaustive study of the Torah. For nowhere else can they locate themselves in history, or learn what God demands of them.

(Throughout the present study, *traditionalists* means *traditionalist Jewish commentators,* and *traditionalism* means *Jewish traditionalism.*)

The fact central to the study is that, in a significant number of instances, perhaps even typically, as regards both sacred history and codex, the plain meaning of the Pentateuch is impossible to understand; basically because, whenever God, so to speak, wants to, He uses language to preclude understanding; in the sacred history by describing events in language that supports, often, perhaps even typically, a multitude of equally plausible meanings, and in the codex by mandating law in language that supports, often, perhaps even typically, equally plausible but irreconcilable mandates, usually two of them.

In the opinion of the present study, traditionalism necessitates two related responses to the fact above: that, in a significant number of instances, perhaps even typically, inquiry can prompt only plausible speculation, not certainty: that is to say, not truth, defined as the position that exists in the mind, or in the will, so to speak, of God; and that a counter-response to the fact that derives from a view of reality antithetical to that of traditionalism, when focused upon a theological question that, though not (except in one opinion, regarding a specific group of laws in the codex) interdicted, perforce yields nothing of value to traditionalism.

That the fact central to the study exists cannot be attributed to errors in the text of the Pentateuch, because it was revealed by the only Author who is, axiomatically, incapable of error, or to defects of transmission or editing, because it is axiomatic that God intended, and traditionalists have therefore perforce assured, that it never be marred by corruption. That is to say, to traditionalists the fact central to the present study must bespeak the intent of the Author to embed in the Pentateuch, in a significant number of places, perhaps even typically, the motif of *mysterium*, of incomprehensibility. And, as He is perfect, He must have written a perfect book; and that has always been, and always will be, the book traditionalists study and revere.

That a God who is essentially incomprehensible should have done that is not, as a theological matter, problematic to traditionalists; and neither are two related responses necessitated by what He did: to acknowledge that, often, perhaps even typically, the Pentateuch precludes not inquiry, but certainty about the conclusions inquiry prompts; and to be, at the minimum, wary of a counter-response to the fact derived from a view of reality antithetical to that of traditionalism. Traditionalism encourages almost unlimited inquiry, and tolerates even inquiry rooted in the view of reality noted that is antithetical to its own; but stipulates, in the opinion of the present study, that often, perhaps even typically, the conclusions prompted are of value only as plausible speculation; a stipulation that applies to all inquiry about the Pentateuch except inquiry about a specific set of laws that either must not, or may not (opinions differ), be thought about, but that, as regards a theological question of no moment to traditionalism, in the opinion of an esteemed modern traditionalist and of the present study, is valueless because perforce vain, or—the equivalent word—futile.

That traditionalists have accepted the freedom of inquiry noted, and, as a theological matter, the stipulation noted, is evident. That they have, as a practical matter, accepted the stipulation, is not evident. Traditionalists discuss without hesitation virtually every event in sacred history recorded in the Pentateuch, and every law in its codex. And all of them affirm, as theologians, that because God is impenetrably Other, His book must be, in some significant measure, perhaps even typically, impervious to understanding. As a practical matter, however, they typically presume that little, if anything, is beyond their understanding, and therefore typically explicate, with apparent confidence, virtually every word of the Pentateuch. Their deference to *mysterium* notwithstanding, they typically trust their minds to understand, more or less completely, God's book, without much noting that their conclusions are often, perhaps even typically, perforce nothing more than plausible speculation.

But that trust may hinder, rather than promote, understanding. If *mysterium* is not only a theological fact, but, as will be shown, at the minimum a significant impression, and perhaps even a pervasive impression, that must result from a productive encounter with the Pentateuch—if, that is to say, it is a dictum almost never asserted explicitly in the text, but an unavoidable conclusion often, perhaps even typically, implicit in its language—traditionalists should be persuaded to trust their minds to speak with certainty less than they typically do. They should, in other words, be persuaded that, in some significant measure, perhaps even typically, accepting that a limitation of thought is, in the Pentateuch's view of reality, inherent in the human condition yields deeper understanding than does thought itself.

As will be shown, persuading them of that necessitates persuading them that their apparent confidence about the power of thought to yield certainty derives from a view of reality that is antithetical to their own, and that obscures, rather than illuminates, their understanding of the Pentateuch, and therefore of the view of reality the Pentateuch defines.

In the introduction below, to underscore the fact central to the present study, a brief analysis shows that language is sometimes used to preclude understanding of the sacred history narrated in the Nineteenth and Twentieth Chapters of the Book of Exodus. Then the study shows that language is similarly used in significant, perhaps even in pervasive, degree, throughout the Pentateuch, in the sacred history it narrates, and in the law it expounds. The study thus demonstrates that *mysterium* is a significant, perhaps even a pervasive, motif in the Pentateuch, and argues that in consequence traditionalism must be grounded, as a practical as well as a theoretical matter, not in a conviction, essentially antithetical to it, that the human mind intelligent enough and well enough disciplined can understand all of reality, but in the contrary conviction that, to a significant, perhaps even to a pervasive, degree, reality cannot be understood.

༄

The Nineteenth and Twentieth Chapters of the Book of Exodus appear to begin recounting the seminal event of sacred history—the experience by the Jews of Revelation at Mount Sinai—in a straightforward, unambiguous narrative. In fact, however, so many difficulties are embedded in the narrative that the more closely it is looked at, the more, to at least a significant degree, perhaps even typically, it precludes understanding.

The first two verses, for example, 19:1-2, seem to contain too many words. In Kaplan's translation they read as follows:

> [1] In the third month after the Israelites left Egypt, on the first of the month, they came to the desert of Sinai. [2] They had departed

from Rephidim and had arrived in the Sinai Desert, camping in the wilderness. Israel camped opposite the mountain.

Recast more succinctly, the two verses would read as follows:

[1] In the third month after the Israelites left Egypt, on the first of the month, they came to the Sinai Desert. [2] They camped there, in the wilderness, opposite the mountain.

There seems no need to repeat in 19:2 the assertion in 19:1 that the Jews came to the Sinai Desert. (Kaplan's substitutions—of "arrived" for "came," of "Sinai Desert" for "the desert of Sinai," and of "wilderness" for "desert"—are misleading. In none of the three instances do the Hebrew words change. And Kaplan does not translate "there," the Hebrew *sham*.) There seems no need either to state that the Jews had come from Rephidim, because that was stated in Exodus 17:1. And the reference to "*the* mountain" is not clear, because the definite article presumes an antecedent, but none exists. An unusually retentive reader may recall that when Moses spoke with God at the burning bush, on "God's Mountain, in the Horeb area," (3:1) he was told that after the Exodus the Jews would "become God's servants on this mountain," (3:12) and that later Moses was visited by his father-in-law in "the desert . . . near God's mountain." (18:5) But most readers will recall neither reference; in any case, neither can be called an antecedent; and it is by no means clear that "God's mountain" is "the mountain" mentioned in 19:2.

In 19:3, God's instruction to Moses—"This is what you must say to the family of Jacob and tell the Israelites"—seems to contain too many words. Either "the family of Jacob" or "the Israelites" would seem sufficient.

In 19:5, Moses is instructed to tell the Jews:

"Now if you obey Me and keep My covenant, you shall be My special treasure among all nations, even though all the world is Mine."

This verse contains two difficulties. First, it is not clear what the difference, if any, is between "obey Me" and "keep My covenant," because obedience would appear to consist solely in keeping God's covenant, and therefore it is not clear what God intends by "obey Me." This difficulty would be eliminated by translating the Hebrew as, "Now if you obey Me by keeping My covenant." But that translation would not be faithful to the Hebrew. Moreover, it is not clear what covenant God is referring to, because He has never mentioned to the Jews a covenant with them. Second, a lacuna seems to exist in 19:5. Moses is instructed to tell the Jews that, if they keep God's covenant, they will be His "special treasure among all nations, even though all the world is Mine." Kaplan follows Ibn Ezra in rendering the Hebrew *ki* as "even though." Even that unusual rendering indicates that, at the minimum, words are missing that are necessary to connect "all the world is mine" to the rest of God's statement. The more usual rendering of *ki*, "because," underscores the disconnect.

The closing instruction in 19:6—"These are the words that you [Moses] must relate to the Israelites"—seems unnecessary. It seems simply to repeat 19:3—"This is what you must say to the family of Jacob and tell the Israelites." And by omitting "the family of Jacob" it underscores that the appearance of those words in 19:3 seems unnecessary.

Because God has instructed Moses to convey His message "to the Israelites"—that is to say, to the entire nation—it is not clear why, in 19:7, Moses summons only "the elders of the people," or why, in 19:8, not they but "all the people answered as one."

The difficulty, in 19:9, in God's assertion that the spoken Revelation will be addressed only to Moses cannot be immediately recognized. God tells him:

> "I will come to *you* in a thick cloud, so that all the people will hear when I speak to *you*."[emphasis added]

The spoken Revelation begins, in 20:1, with an assertion—"God spoke all these words"—that does not specify who is being addressed. The Ten Pronouncements (not "Commandments," a different Hebrew word) are expressed in the singular, and therefore may be addressed only to Moses, not to all of the Jews. At some unspecified moment—whether before, during, or after the spoken Revelation is not clear—the Jews, terrified, beg Moses, in 20:16, "You speak to us, and we will listen. But let God not speak with us any more, for we will die if He does." (The words "any more" in Kaplan's translation do not appear in the Hebrew text. Ramban, in his commentary on 20:15, says they should not be inserted.) But after the Pronouncements are made, God reminds the Jews, through Moses, in 20:19, that "I spoke to you from heaven," "you" being *emachem*, the plural in Hebrew. (It is used again in Deuteronomy 5:4, when Moses reminds the Jews that at the Revelation "God spoke to you, face to face.") Thus, it may not be not possible to know to whom God addresses the Ten Pronouncements.

Nor may it be possible to know whether the Jews even hear the Pronouncements. God asserts that "all the people will hear when I speak to you." But it is not clear from 20:15-16 whether they hear (and see) anything more than the turmoil on Mount Sinai:

> [15] All the people saw the sounds, the flames, the blast of the ram's horn, and the mountain smoking. The people trembled when they saw it, keeping their distance. [16] They said to Moses, "You speak to us, and we will listen. But let God not speak to us any more, for we will die if He does."

The Jews are terrified enough by the sounds, the flames, the blast of the ram's horn and the smoking of the mountain to tremble, and to keep their distance; they sense they will not be able to bear the additional terror of hearing God speak; and therefore they beg Moses to listen in their behalf. That is the plain meaning of the text, unless the turmoil persists while God speaks. If it does, the Jews may be terrified by the combination of the turmoil and hearing God speak. That, it seems, must be the case, because God says the Jews will hear Him speaking to Moses. But whether or not they do is not clear. Neither is it clear whether the turmoil of the mountain terrifies them before, while, or after the Pronouncements are spoken.

The assertion, in 19:9, that "Moses told God the people's response" to the offer made by Him in 19:4-6 seems unnecessary, because it seems to repeat the assertion in 19:8 that "Moses brought the people's response back to God."

The assertion in 19:13 that anyone who touches the mountain during the Revelation will be killed can be translated in so many ways, it is not possible to know what it means. Kaplan translates it, "You will not have to lay a hand on him, for he will be stoned or cast down." But as he notes, the Hebrew can also be translated in the following ways:

> **You will not have to . . .**(*Targum Yonathan*). Or, "Do not touch him with your hand" (*Lekach Tov;* Rashbam; Ibn Ezra; Baaley Tosafoth). Or, "Let no hand touch [the mountain]" (*Mekhilta*).

> **cast down.** (*Sanhedrin* 45a; Rashi; *MeAm Lo'ez;* cf: Malbim; Hirsch). Or, "he shall be stoned or shot [with an arrow]" (Rashbam; Ibn Ezra; Bachya; Abarbanel; cf. 2 Chronicles 26:15) or, "He will be stoned or killed with lightning bolts" (*Targum Yonathan*). Others, "Let no man touch [the mountain] with his hand, for he must then be put to death by stoning [after being] thrown down" (Mekhilta; Sanhedrin 45a) See 21:31, Leviticus 4:23.

Because every one of the translations above is faithful to the Hebrew, it is not possible to know which of them conveys the plain meaning of the text; or, indeed, if any of them does.

The assertion, in 19:13, that the prohibition against touching the mountain will end when "the trumpet is sounded with a long blast" seems to mean the Jews may touch the mountain in 19:16, when "an extremely loud blast of a ram's horn" is heard. But in 19:21 they are reminded "not to cross the boundary" because doing so "will cause many to die." Though Kaplan translates *ha'yovel* as "trumpet" and *shofar* as "ram's horn," other traditionalists translate both words as "ram's horn," as Kaplan indicates in a footnote. Thus it is not clear whether the Jews could have touched the mountain once the ram's horn had sounded, or even (to translate 19:13 more accurately than Kaplan does) *b'emshoch ha'yovel*, while the ram's horn is sounding. Neither is it clear why 19:13 and 19:19 refer, respectively, to *ha'yovel*, to *the* trumpet, and to *ha'shofar*, to *the* ram's horn, because no antecedent exists for either reference, whereas 19:20 refers to *a* ram's horn.

The command to the Jews regarding the mountain is accompanied by two other commands, both problematic. Moses is instructed, in 19:12, somehow to "sanctify" the Jews; but how he must do that is not clear. And he must warn them about the mountain; but neglects, it seems, to do so.

His apparent neglect is puzzling, for three reasons. First, God commanded him to issue the warning. Second, it is a matter of life and death. And third, when the Revelation begins, God and Moses seem to speak at cross-purposes. God's instruction to Moses, in 19:21, already noted, to "warn the people that they must not cross the boundary . . . because this will cause many to die" seems to presume that Moses has not yet issued that warning. Moses, however, insists, in 19:23, that God Himself issued it: "You already warned them to set a boundary around the mountain and to declare it sacred." But God, it seems, did no such thing; He ordered Moses to issue the warning, and Moses, it seems, did not issue it.

To the concerns regarding sacred history noted thus far, the general response of secular critics is unobjectionable. As the text of Exodus is, in their opinion, a composite work, written over centuries by a number of authors, and edited in a similarly collective fashion, concerns of all sorts inevitably exist; and the task of criticism is in consequence by various means to establish a standard text, and to analyze the concerns that exist in it by analyzing the cultures in which it evolved; in particular, their philosophical, religious, aesthetic, and linguistic presumptions. In this view, the Book of Exodus is no different from, say, *The Odyssey*, a work fashioned slowly over time by human beings rooted in particular cultures, and therefore, however impressive, inevitably flawed.

To traditionalists such a view is unacceptable, because it conflicts with the theological axiom, noted above, upon which all of traditionalism is founded: that the Book of Exodus, like the rest of the Pentateuch, was dictated by God to Moses during the Revelation at Mount Sinai, some thirty-five hundred years ago, and has been preserved uncorrupted since then by divine decree effected by traditionalists.

In this view, the Pentateuch is different in kind from any book that exists, or can exist. Because it was written by an omniscient and benevolent God as a comprehensive guide to sacred history and to conduct, it must be a perfect work; the only work, indeed, that can be imagined in which intention and execution are perforce identical; that is to say, in which the Author knew precisely what He wanted to say, and said it precisely as He intended to. And because He loves Jews in particular as a father loves his children, His basic intention must have been to edify them.

This view of the book, formulated classically by Maimonides, and epitomized in the contemporary statement below, has been the cornerstone of traditionalism for at least the past sixteen hundred years, from the time the Talmud,[3] the work that interprets the Torah, was redacted to the present:

> Maimonides, or *Rambam*, formulated the Thirteen Principles of Faith, which are incumbent upon every Jew. Two of them, the eight and the ninth, refer to the Torah. As they have been set down briefly in the familiar text of *Ani Maamin*, they are:
>
> 8. I believe with complete faith that the entire Torah now in our hands is the same one that was given to Moses, our teacher, peace be upon him.
>
> 9. I believe with complete faith that this Torah will not be exchanged, nor will there be another Torah from the Creator, Blessed is His Name.
>
> These principles are essential parts of the faith of the Jew, and they are also fundamental to the way one studies the Torah. For the attitude of one who approaches a book as the immutable word of God is far, far different from that of one who holds a volume that was composed by men and emended by others over the years. As we begin the study of the Torah, we should resolve

---

3. All references except p. 142 are to the Babylonian Talmud.

> that this recognition of its origin and immutability will be in our consciousness always.
>
> In several of his writings, *Rambam* sets forth at much greater length the unanimously held view that every letter and word of the Torah was given to Moses by God; that it has not been and cannot be changed; and that nothing was ever or can ever be added to it. Indeed, the Talmud states emphatically that if one questions the Divine origin of even a single letter or traditionally accepted interpretation of the Torah, it is tantamount to denial of the entire Torah (*Sanhedrin 99a*).
>
> This harsh judgment is quite proper, for if a critic can take it upon himself to deny the provenance of one verse or letter of the Torah, what is to stop him from discarding any part that displeases him? Modern times illustrate this all too clearly. And logic dictates that man cannot tamper with the word of God, not merely because man's intelligence is of a different, infinitely inferior order, but because God and His wisdom are perfect, and, by definition, perfection cannot be improved....
>
> Throughout history, Jews have maintained the absolute integrity of their Torah scrolls, zealously avoiding any change, even of a letter that would not change the meaning of a word. They knew that their Torah was not merely a "sacred book," it was the word of God, and as such it had to remain unchanged.[4]

The assertion that questioning "even a single letter or traditionally accepted interpretation of the Torah" amounts to "denial of the entire Torah" needs to be explained. Otherwise, the statement above is a theologically unexceptionable *credo*. Traditionalism accepts, as an act of faith, that the Pentateuch is a perfect work, dictated in its entirety by God to Moses at Mount Sinai, its absolute integrity uncorrupted since that seminal moment in history because of the zeal of traditionalists in effecting God's intention that it not be corrupted. Therefore the task of traditionalism differs from, and is more difficult than, that of secular commentary. Both disciplines expound the Pentateuch. But traditionalists cannot be concerned with cultural anthropology, because they presume the Pentateuch did not evolve, but erupted, complete, from the Godhead, at Mount Sinai. And because they presume that it erupted perfect, they cannot presume that it is in any way flawed.

But that it seems to be flawed is evident, as even the close reading above of a short excerpt from Exodus shows, and as close readings of

---

4. *The Chumash* [the Pentateuch] (New York: 2002), pp. xix-xx.

various sections of the Pentateuch, chosen at random, show. And therein lies the especial difficulty of traditionalism. The secularist can argue imperfection; the traditionalist cannot. And so traditionalists must presume, often in the face of apparently formidable evidence to the contrary, either that concerns regarding the text can be resolved, completely or in part, or that they are mysteries that perforce prove impervious to understanding.

Traditionalism is usually represented by, among others, Rashi, Ramban, Sforno, Saadia Gaon, Ibn Ezra, Chizkuni, Rashbam, Meam Loez, Abarbanel, Malbim, Baal Haturim, Siftei Chachomim, Rabbenu Bachya, Or Hachayim, Alshich, Daat Mikrah, Kli Yakar, and Midrash. But the volume and the range of related readings are vast; not only traditionalists have considered the concerns contained in Exodus 18 and 19, and in other sections of the Pentateuch to be discussed; concerns they have not discussed have been discussed elsewhere; and so the present study does not intend to be complete. But it need not be, to fulfill its objectives: to demonstrate the inherent intellectual limitation of traditionalism, to suggest that the limitation is a major strength, to reconcile traditionalists to the suggestion, and to caution them about the futility of studying traditionalism by reference to a view of reality antithetical to it.

Their disinclination to consider, as a practical matter, efforts to demonstrate the inherent limitation, not of inquiry itself, but of the knowledge, as opposed to the plausible speculation, it can provide is understandable, because, they believe, the Pentateuch, illuminated by the Talmud (the Mishnah, and the commentary upon it, the Gemara) is the only absolutely reliable guide to sacred history and to conduct, and because in consequence in proportion as they cannot understand its plain meaning, they cannot understand, to a certainty, their history, or know how to live.

The inherent intellectual limitation of traditionalist inquiry into sacred history may be underscored by its response to the concerns in the two chapters of Exodus discussed briefly above.

About how to explain two details of the seeming wordiness of 19:1-2 traditionalists differ.

As several of them note, the first three of the four verbs in 19:1-2 are in the plural, whereas the fourth, which repeats "camped," is in the singular. Thus, the Jews "came" (*ba'u*) to Mount Sinai, having "travelled" (*va'yisu*) from Refidim, and "camped" (*va'yachanu*) in the desert. But they "camped" (*va'yichan*) near the mountain. On how to explain the grammatical shift opinions differ. Rashi explains it by asserting that the Jews stand at the mountain "as one person with one heart"—that is, to say, in perfect unity. Ibn Ezra explains that the second "camped" refers to the leaders of the Jews, who camp nearer to the mountain than do the others, and who are so few in number they are referred to in the singular. Ramban suggests that the second "camped" may show that the Jews had separated themselves from the *eirev rav*, the "mixed multitude" of non-Jews who had gone out of Egypt with them.

Because none of the opinions above is supported by evidence in the text, and because in consequence any one of them may be preferred to the other two, or all three may be disregarded, it is not possible, having read them, to explain the shift from plural to singular.

About the repetition of "Refidim" opinions also differ. Rashi, referencing Mechilta, notes that, because the arrival of the Jews at Refidim is mentioned in Exodus 17:1, and because they journeyed from there to the Sinai Desert, it seems unnecessary to mention in 19:1 that they journeyed from Refidim. In the opinion of Mechilta, it is mentioned to show that just as, having rebelled against God at Refidim, they repented, so they approach Mount Sinai repentant. In the opinion of Chizkuni, there is no evidence that they did repent at Refidim. In the opinion of Ramban, because the text uses the formulaic language "They journeyed from . . . and camped at" when recounting the journeys of the Jews in Numbers 33:1-49, no inference regarding repentance should be drawn from the use of the same language in Exodus 19:2. And if they did repent at Rifidim, it is not clear for what sin they are repenting when they stand at Mount Sinai.

Opinions regarding 19:3—"This is what you must say (*to'mar*) to the family of Jacob and tell (*ve'tageid*) the Israelites"—are so various, it is not possible to know what the verse means. Rashi conflates two readings in Mechilta: that "the family of Jacob" (*le'beit yaacov*) refers to the women, and "the Israelites" (*livnei yisrael*) refers to the men; and that the gentleness of *to'mar* as a tone of address differs from the stringency of tone of *ve'tageid*. Mechilta simply records both readings. Malbim asserts that "the family of Jacob" refers to most of the Jews, whereas "the Israelites" refers to Jews of high spiritual standing. Ibn Ezra asserts that "the Israelites" refers to "the elders" (*hazkeinim*), the communal leaders (*ziknei ha'awm*) to whom Moses conveys God's message in 19:7. Chizkuni asserts that *tomar* refers to future events, whereas *vuhtahgade* refers to the recounting of history.

To account for the second of the seeming repetitions in 19:3—"Now if you obey Me and keep My covenant"—Ibn Ezra, Malbim, and Sforno assert that "obey Me" refers to obeying God's commandments, whereas "keep My covenant" refers to living up to some unspecified covenant God and the Jews will enter into after He has made the Ten Pronouncements. In the opinion of Mechilta, "obey Me" refers to obeying God's commandments, whereas "keep my covenant" refers to obeying specific commandments; in Rabbi Eliezer's view, to observe the Sabbath; in Rabbi Akiva's, to practice circumcision and to avoid idolatry. Ramban, Rashi, and Or Hachayim focus on one of the two phrases, and thus do not openly acknowledge that a repetition exists. Ramban asserts that "keep My covenant" refers to the covenant that God made with Abraham in Genesis 17:4-14, and thus implies that "obey Me" refers to some unspecified commitment to be made by the Jews, perhaps at Mount Sinai. Rashi agrees with Ibn Ezra that "keep My covenant" refers to living up to some unspecified contract God and the Jews will enter into after He has made the Ten Pronouncements. But unlike Ibn Ezra, he does not comment on "obey Me." Or Hachayim, responding to the literal translation of *shamoah tischmehu*—not "obey Me," but "listen, listen"—asserts that the first "listen" refers to the Written Torah, and the second to the Oral Torah, and thus that "obey Me" in Kaplan's translation refers to obeying God's commandments.

If it were permissible to edit the text, the seeming lacuna in 19:5 could be dealt with by moving "even though all the earth is Mine" and adding a few words to 19:6, so that the passage would read as follows:

> "Now if you obey Me and keep My covenant, you shall be My special treasure among all nations, a kingdom of priests and a holy nation to Me. I can arrange that, because all the world is Mine, and therefore I can do as I wish."

Because, however, traditionalists believe that the text cannot be edited, it resists understanding. In the opinion of Rashi, the lacuna indicates that God does not love non-Jews. In the opinion of Mechilta, Sforno, Ramban, and Or Hachayim, it forestalls the mistaken impression that God loves only the Jews, but emphasizes that His love for them is unique in intensity and in kind.

Commenting on the seeming redundancy of the closing instruction in 19:6—"These are the words that you [Moses] must relate to the Israelites"—Rashi, following Mechilta, explains that it charges Moses to say neither less nor more than God has commanded him to say. Malbim asserts that the closing instruction refers only to the closing words of 19:6; that is, that Moses is to convey all of God's words to all of the Jews, with the exception of "You will be a kingdom of priests and a holy nation to Me," which only the men are to hear.

Opinions differ about why, though instructed to convey God's message to all of the Jews, Moses summons the elders, and why not they but all of the Jews respond to the offer from God that he conveys. In the opinion of Mechilta, Moses summons the elders to show his respect for them; and then presumably goes with them to the other Jews. In the opinion of Or Hachayim, he goes first to the elders because he is afraid the other Jews will not accept God's offer, and needs the assurance that acceptance by the elders will provide. In the opinion of Malbim, Moses separates the Jews into groups, by degrees of spiritual elevation, then addresses each group separately. In the opinion of Chizkuni, he summons the elders simply to accompany him. (Therefore 19:7 should perhaps read not, as in Kaplan's translation, "Moses . . . summoned the elders of the people, conveying to them all that God had spoken," but "Moses summoned . . . the elders, and in their company conveyed to the people all that God had spoken.")

The variety of equally plausible opinions about whether, during the spoken Revelation, God is addressing Moses, all of the Jews, or both, makes it difficult—perhaps impossible—to choose between them. As noted, God proposes to speak only to Moses—"I will come to *you*" and "speak to *you*"—then speaks to an unspecified audience—"God spoke all these words"—then perhaps addresses the Ten Pronouncements, all rendered in the singular, to Moses only, but then asserts that He has spoken to all of the Jews. When who heard what, and when, is considered, even the most careful reader may well not be able to prefer any of the answers proposed to the others; or, indeed, to conclude that any of them explains what happened.

In the opinion of Rashi, who references Mechilta, commenting on 20:1—"God spoke all these words, saying"—all of the Jews hear the Ten Pronouncements, uttered by God in a single instant, and bind themselves verbally to obey each Pronouncement. In the opinion of Sforno, who references Deuteronomy 5:19—"God spoke these words in a loud voice to your entire assembly from the mountain"—all of the Jews hear all of the Pronouncements. In the opinion shared by Ramban, in his commentary on 20:7, and by Rambam (Moreh Hanevuchim 2:32), the Jews hear only the first two pronouncements directly from God, and are taught the other eight by Moses.

When the Jews, terrified, draw back from the mountain is a matter of dispute. In Ibn Ezra's opinion, in 20:17, they do so when they hear

God speaking. Rashi agrees, asserting that in 20:15—"All of the people saw the sounds, the flames, the blast of the ram's horn, and the mountain smoking"—"the sounds" refers to God's words. In Ramban's opinion, in 20:15, they draw back in terror before God utters the Pronouncements.

Opinions differ about how to explain the seeming repetition in 19:9. Rashi says that, to complement their message to God, in 19:8, the Jews send another: that they want to hear God's Pronouncements directly from Him, not through Moses. Malbim distinguishes between "brought . . . back" (*va'yasheiv*) in "Moses brought the people's response back to God" and "told" (*va'yageid*) in "Moses told the people God's response." *Va'yasheiv*, he says, refers to the response of the Jews to God's offer, whereas *va'yageid* refers to some new matter; in this case, the Jews' wish to experience prophesy at Moses' level. In the opinion of Ibn Ezra, *va'yageid* refers to the response that Moses had already brought back to God in 19:8. In Ramban's opinion, *va'yasheiv* refers to Moses' intention—he goes back to God in order to tell Him the Jews' response—whereas *va'yagaeid* refers to what he does—he tells Him.

About the function and the identity of the ram's horn opinion is also divided. Following Mechilta, Rashi asserts that the Jews may not approach the mountain until a loud blast from the ram's horn is sounded, the sign that the Divine has departed. Malbim asserts that, had they not been terrified (because they were spiritually weak), they could have approached the mountain while the ram's horn was sounding; indeed, they could have ascended the mountain with Moses, and have experienced Revelation as he did. In Rashbam's opinion, *bimshoch ha'yovel* should be translated not as "while the ram's horn is sounding," but as "when the ram's horn stops sounding." In the opinion of Saadia Gaon, when the ram's horn sounds, any Jew may ascend the mountain. In the opinion of Ibn Ezra, only when Moses sounds a loud blast on the ram's horn, when he returns from the second or the third (opinions differ) of his forty-day stays on the mountain may the mountain be ascended; but only by Aaron, two of his sons, and seventy designated elders. In the opinion of Chizkuni, referencing Saadia Gaon, any Jew may ascend the mountain; but only when Moses sounds a blast of the ram's horn (not the ram's horn that sounds at Mount Sinai) when the Tabernacle has been erected.

In the opinion of Rashi, the references to *the* trumpet and *the* ram's horn indicate that the ram's horn used at Mount Sinai was taken from the ram Abraham sacrificed in place of Isaac. Baal Haturim agrees, and notes that that ram's horn was used again, by Joshua, to bring down the walls of

Jericho. In the opinion of Ramban, that cannot be, because Abraham must have burned the ram's horn with the rest of its carcass when he sacrificed it in place of Isaac.

Opinion is divided on how the Jews are to be sanctified. Ibn Ezra asserts that Moses is commanded to sanctify them by instructing them to immerse their bodies and their clothing. In the opinion of Ramban and Rashi, he is to instruct the men to refrain from sexual intercourse with their wives. In the opinion of Malbim, to remain eligible to receive the Revelation directly from God, rather than indirectly through Moses, the Jews are to be sanctified by having their souls elevated through a process of spiritual instruction that is not specified, and that the immersion of their bodies and clothing will betoken.

In his commentary on 19:21, Malbim assumes that a first warning not to touch the mountain exists in the text, and explains at length why, just before the spoken Revelation begins, God commands Moses to warn the Jews a second time about the mountain. Rashi's opinion about "warn the people" is ambiguous. It may indicate that Moses is warning them for the first time. But Rashi may simply be commenting on *ha'eid* ("warn"), which means literally "bear witness," to underscore the rabbinic requirement that Jews must be reminded in the presence of witnesses of known dangers when they are imminent.

Because traditionalist inquiry into the two chapters of Exodus discussed briefly and incompletely above is often, perhaps even typically, confronted with a multiplicity of equally plausible responses, often, perhaps even typically, asserted rather than supported by evidence, as that term is usually understood, to puzzling concerns, traditionalists cannot, in the opinion of the present essay, legitimately expect to attain knowledge to a certainty as regards those concerns, but must perforce settle for plausible speculation; their choices among the responses available often, perhaps even typically, matters of taste; and the possibility not discountable that none of their choices establishes the plain meaning of narrative debated.

That is true, for example, as regards the following concerns: why the arrival of the Jews at Rephidim seems to be recounted in too many words, why they are referred to first in the plural, then in the singular, whether or not the Jews repent at Rephidim, what, if anything, they repent of at Mount Sinai, who the family of Jacob and the Jews are, what the difference is between obeying God and keeping His covenant, why Moses addresses the elders, rather than, as commanded, all of the Jews, what covenant God is referring to when He tells Moses to convey His offer to the Jews, why He tells Moses twice to convey the offer, why He does not mention the family of Jacob the second time, how Moses is to sanctify the Jews, which ram's horn is sounded at the mountain, whether Jews who touch the mountain will die, or will ascend it and in consequence see God, how they will die, if they will, when the ram's horn will sound to signify the mountain is no longer dangerous and the Jews may in consequence ascend it, if they may, whether God intends to give the Torah to them directly, or indirectly, through Moses, whom God addresses during the spoken Revelation, when the Jews recoil in terror from the Revelation, how much of the spoken Revelation they hear. About none of these concerns does the Pentateuch speak clearly.

And as that is the case not only as regards the two chapters discussed above, but, as will be shown, as regards other sections chosen at random, and as could be shown, as regards almost every section of the Pentateuch, *mysterium* is a significant, perhaps even a pervasive, motif in the Pentateuch. The two chapters discussed, for example, are part of a single dramatic unit—the Revelation, and the building of the Tabernacle—that occupies the fifty-seven chapters from Exodus 19 to Numbers 9, each of them full of the sorts of concerns relating to sacred history discussed above (and further complicated by concerns, not yet discussed, relating to the exposition of law). And as that dramatic unit is but one of the many, equally complicated, that constitute the Pentateuch, affirming that, to some significant extent, perhaps even typically, the plain meaning of the text is impossible to establish to a certainty is, in the opinion of the present study, an indispensable prerequisite to a productive encounter with it.

That affirmation must be made equally by secular scholars and by traditionalists. But, as noted, it is much more difficult for traditionalists to make, because much more is at stake for them. Secular scholars undertake to study a text similar in kind to all others. Their intent is entirely intellectual: to understand it. Difficult concerns do not surprise them, given their presumptions about how the text evolved. And whether the concerns in fact defy comprehension remains for them an open question, to be answered as knowledge in a variety of relevant disciplines advances. Traditionalists, by contrast, undertake to study the only book ever written by their God, and therefore the only book perforce perfect, transferred from, so to speak, His head to His Chosen People in an instant about which all of history pivots, and during which a sacred history was narrated and a comprehensive code of conduct was expounded. Their intention is essentially theological: to understand the history He directs, and the system of law He mandated, primarily to the Jews, His Chosen People. To the extent that puzzling concerns exist, they cannot understand their history, or how to live. Thus, a sense of seriousness, urgency and anxiety perforce absent from secular scholarship attends their study of the text in general, in proportion as the puzzling concerns prove impervious to understanding.

And that many of them do prove impervious to it is a fact, from which, for traditionalism, there is no refuge. Not all puzzling concerns in the Pentateuch are beyond understanding. But against the significant number at least that are not even two theological dicta invoked, often, and almost formulaically, afford protection. The dictum that many plain meanings of a narrative fact may co-exist (*shivim panim la'torah*) must mean something metaphorically, as must the related dictum that interpretations that seem contradictory may be true (*eilu ve'eilu divrei elokim chayim*). But neither dictum can have literal meaning when a concern regarding historical fact is studied. For example, the ram's horn that signals Mount Sinai may once again be approached cannot be sounded by God when the spoken Revelation ends and by Moses when he returns from the second, or third, of his forty-day stays on the mountain. (Nor, as will be shown, can either dictum have literal meaning when irreconcilable interpretations of the plain meaning of a law are studied.)

Whatever the metaphoric meaning of the two dicta, concerns related to sacred history (and, as will be shown, concerns related to law) that are impervious to understanding constitute a significant, perhaps even a pervasive, motif in the Pentateuch. And that inescapable fact mandates three tasks. The fact must be documented, as regards both sacred history and law. The response the fact compels must be underscored, and discussed effectively enough so that, as a theological and practical matter, traditionalists consider it seriously. And that a counter-response antithetical to traditionalism perforce produces nothing of value to it must be demonstrated.

The first of the three tasks, begun in the analysis above of the Nineteenth and Twentieth chapters of Exodus, continues below, in further discussions of sacred history. Then, in turn, that the motif in the sacred history in the Pentateuch is, at the minimum, significant, and perhaps even pervasive, also in the codex it mandates is demonstrated, the response the fact compels is underscored, and the futility of the counter-response is discussed.

The apparent clarity with which the history of Joseph is narrated masks a wide variety of concerns that make it to some significant degree, perhaps even typically, impossible to understand what happens in two episodes to be discussed, and why Joseph and his brothers act as they do.

The episodes are contained in Genesis 37:1-36, and in 42:1-38. The first recounts the sale of Joseph into slavery in Egypt; the second recounts the first of the journeys into Egypt of his brothers to purchase food, and its aftermath.

The verse that introduces Joseph, 37:2, is problematic for a number of reasons, one of them obscured by Kaplan's legitimate translation:

> These are the chronicles of Jacob: Joseph was 17 years old. As a lad, he would tend the sheep with his brothers, the sons of Bilhah and Zilpah, his father's wives. Joseph brought his father a bad report about them.

A more awkward, but more revealing, translation underscores that it is not possible to integrate into the second sentence the clause highlighted below:

> These are the chronicles of Jacob: Joseph, at 17 years old, would tend the sheep with his brothers, *and he was a lad with the sons of his father's wives Bilhah and Zilpah.* Joseph brought his father a bad report about them.

The highlighted clause may mean that Joseph usually keeps company with the sons of Bilhah and Zilpah, rather than with his other brothers, all of them except Benjamin and Joseph, the sons of their dead mother, Rachel, the sons of Leah. But if that is the case, the plain meaning of the verse is that Joseph tends the sheep with all of his brothers, and brings his father a bad report about all of them, rather than, as Kaplan's translation seems to indicate, that he tends the sheep only with the sons of Bilhah and Zilpah, and brings the bad report only about them. However, if the Hebrew words "and he was a lad" are detached, as they can be, from the rest of the italicized clause, Kaplan's translation conveys the plain meaning of the verse, because it is then legitimate to regard "the sons of Bilhah and Zilpah, his father's wives" as in apposition to "with his brothers." But if the words are detached, they can be moved only to the vicinity of "Joseph was 17 years old," where they seem (as in Kaplan's translation) to be redundant, because a boy of seventeen is obviously "a lad."

The opening words of 37:2, and the nature of the report Joseph brings to his father, are also problematic.

The opening words—"These are the chronicles of Jacob"—are puzzling, because they introduce the chronicles not of Jacob, but of Joseph; and especially puzzling when compared to the opening words of 36:1—"These are the chronicles of Esau, also known as Edom"—that introduce the long detailed chronicle of Jacob's brother that immediately precedes 37:2.

What the "bad report" contains is not specified. And whether the brothers know it exists, or what it contains, is not clear.

Why 37:3 asserts that Jacob "loved Joseph more than any of his other sons, because he was the child of his old age" is not clear, because, as Meam Loez notes, the child of his old age is Benjamin, because Naftali, Gad, and Issachar are only about a year older than Joseph, because Zebulun and Joseph are almost the same age (or, as one tradition asserts, Zebulun is younger than Joseph), and because all of the brothers seem to have been born within six or seven years.

If the brothers know about the "bad report," it is not clear why "they began to hate" Joseph in 37:4 only because Jacob loves him more than he loves them, rather than also because they resent the report. (Nor is it clear how many of them might be expected to resent the report, because, as noted, it is not clear how many of them the report censures.)

Because to 37:8 Joseph has related only one dream (*chalom*), it is not clear why 37:8 asserts that his brothers hated him "even more because of his dreams (*chalomtav*) and his words." Nor is it clear what the phrase "his words" refers to, since he seems to have spoken to them only of his dream.

Because Joseph's mother, Rachel, is dead, it is not clear why, having heard Joseph's second dream, Jacob includes her in his question in 37:10, "Do you want me, your mother, and your brothers to come and prostrate ourselves on the ground to you?"

The two assertions that constitute 37:11—"His brothers became very jealous of him, but his father suspended judgment"—are problematic in several regards. Why the brothers become jealous of Joseph only in 37:11 is not clear. Why hatred, which they feel from 37:4, leads to jealousy, rather than the reverse, is not clear. And the relation between the two assertions in 37:11 is problematic; especially because Kaplan's translations are cryptic, and because, as will be seen, more literal translations are vague. That being the case, the relation between the two assertions is unclear. Jacob seems worried about the consequence of the brothers' jealousy. But what precisely he is worried about is not clear.

Jacob's charge to Joseph in 37:12-14 seems to contain too many words:

[12] [Joseph's] brothers left to tend their father's sheep in Shechem. [13] Israel said to Joseph, "I believe your brothers are keeping the sheep in Shechem. I would like you to go to them." "I'm ready," replied Joseph. [14] "Then see how your brothers and the sheep are doing," said [Israel]. "Bring me a report." [Israel] thus sent him from the Hebron valley, and [Joseph] arrived in Shechem.

Recast more succinctly, the charge would read as follows:

[12] [Joseph's] brothers left to tend their father's sheep in Shechem. [13] Israel said to Joseph, "[Go] see how your brothers and the sheep are doing. [14] Bring me a report." [Israel] thus sent him from Hebron valley, and [Joseph] arrived in Shechem.

Joseph's journey, in 37:15-17, towards his brothers is problematic in several regards; indeed, it is essentially mysterious.

[15] A stranger found him blundering about in the fields. "What are you looking for?" asked the stranger. [16] "I'm looking for my brothers," replied [Joseph]. "Perhaps you can tell me where they are tending the sheep." [17] "They already left this area," said the man. "I heard them planning to go to Dothan." Joseph went after his brothers and found them in Dothan.

The encounter of Joseph with "a man"(*ish*, not, as in Kaplan's translation, "a stranger") is puzzling per se, and in its details. It is not clear why the encounter is mentioned. Nor is it clear who the man is, why Joseph is blundering about in the fields, and what the import is of his conversation with the man.

The encounter at Dothan is problematic in several regards. How many of the brothers want to murder Joseph is not clear. Nor is it clear why they are easily dissuaded, by Reuben, and afterwards by Judah, why Reuben and Judah want to dissuade them, what the brothers, having cast Joseph into a dry well, plan to do with him, who removes Joseph from the dry well, who buys him, who transports him to Egypt, and who sells him into slavery there. Finally, it is not clear why, after Joseph is thrown into the well, Reuben suddenly disappears, and reappears after Joseph has been sold.

When the brothers see Joseph approaching, in 37:20, some of them at least want him dead.

"Here comes the dreamer," they said to one another. "Now we have the chance! Let's kill him and throw him into one of the wells. We can say that a wild beast ate him. Then let's see what will become of his dreams!"

That Reuben, who immediately objects in 37:21-22, and Judah, who objects in 37:26-27, are not among the would-be murderers, is clear. But it is not clear who the conspirators are who speak "to one another," or why, having said, in 37:20, "Let's kill him," they are dissuaded, almost without effort, first, by nothing more than Reuben's assertion, in 37:21, "Let's not kill him!" and by his suggestion, in 37:22, that contains no plan of action alternative to murder, that Joseph be thrown into the well; and afterwards, by Judah's rhetorical question in 37:26, "What will we gain if we kill our brother and cover his blood?" Nor is it clear why Reuben and Judah object to the proposed murder, because, as noted, they hate Joseph apparently as much as the other brothers do, and apparently are as jealous of him. The assertion in 37:22 that Reuben's "plan was to rescue [Joseph] from [his brothers] and bring him back to his father" does not explain why Reuben wants to do that. And Judah's question underscores his rhetorical cunning, but does not explain why he does not want Joseph murdered.

That, having thrown Joseph into the well, the brothers still want to murder him is clear from Judah's question to them. But why he nonetheless easily convinces them, in 37:27, to sell him is not clear.

Neither who removes Joseph from the well, nor who sells him to whom, is clear. While the brothers are eating, in 37:25, they see "an Arab caravan" (*ohrchat yishme'eilim*) passing by, and accept Judah's advice, in 37:27, to sell Joseph "to the Arabs (*la'yishme'eilim*)." Kaplan's translation in both verses is misleading; the Hebrew speaks of "a caravan of Ishmaelites" and "to the Ishmaelites." The difference is important, because in 37:28 the following event occurs:

> The strangers, who turned out to be Midianite traders, approached, and [the brothers] pulled Joseph out of the well. They sold him to the Arabs for twenty pieces of silver. [These Midianite Arabs] were to bring Joseph to Egypt.

This translation also is misleading. Translated literally, 37:28 reads as follows:

> Midianite men, merchants, approached. They pulled and lifted Joseph out of the well. They sold Joseph to the Ishmaelites for twenty pieces of silver. They brought him to Egypt.

In this translation, a second group of Arabs, Midianites, approaches the brothers. And the first two uses of "they" are problematic. The first makes it impossible to determine whether the brothers or the Midianites lift Joseph out of the well; so it is impossible to determine whether the brothers or the Midianites sell Joseph to the Ishmaelites. If the brothers perform both actions, it is difficult to understand why the Midianites are mentioned. And if the Midianites perform both actions, it is difficult to understand why the brothers, who have accepted Judah's advice, in 37:27, to sell Joseph to the Ishmaelites, do not object. And the assertion, not that the Ishmaelites "were to bring" Joseph to Egypt, but that in fact they "brought him" (*va'yavi'u*) there, seems contradicted by the assertion, in 37:36, that "The Midanites," seemingly a third group of Arabs, "sold [Joseph] in Egypt to Potiphar, one of Pharaoh's officers, captain of the guard."

Finally, because all of the brothers are present when Joseph arrives at Dothan, and participate in all of the events there, it is not clear why 37:29 asserts that when "Reuben returned to the well, Joseph was no longer there." He must leave sometime after Joseph arrives; but when, and why, where he goes, and why he returns when he does, are not clear.

The two verses that introduce the journey of the brothers into Egypt to purchase food seem to contain too many words, and two words difficult to understand.

The two verses, 42:1-2, read as follows:

> [1] Jacob learned (*va'yar*) that there were provisions in Egypt, and he said to his sons, "Why are you fantasizing (*titra'u*)?" [2] "I have heard (*shamati*) that there are supplies in Egypt," he explained. "You can go there and buy food. Let us live and not die."

Rendered more succinctly, they would read as follows:

> [1] Jacob learned that there were provisions in Egypt, and he said to his sons, "Why are you fantasizing? [2] You can go there and buy food. Let us live and not die."

There seems to be no need for the words removed from 42:2.

The verb that opens 42:1, *va'yar*, means, not "learned," as in Kaplan's translation, but "saw." Why the verb that seems to be appropriate, and that appears in 42:2, *shamati*, does not appear in 42:1 is not clear. Nor is it clear what the question that closes 42:1 means, because it is not clear that *titra'u* means fantasizing.

The assertion in 42:5 that the brothers journey to Egypt "because of the famine in Canaan" does not seem necessary, because it seems to repeat the assertion in 41:56 that "the famine was [also] growing more severe in the entire area." At the minimum, "because of the famine in Canaan" should, it seems, be placed at the beginning of 42:1, the verse that immediately follows 41:56, so as to explain why Jacob speaks to his sons. But if it that were done, the seeming repetition would be underscored in an almost embarrassing fashion, because in the Hebrew (though not in Kaplan's translation) 41:56 closes with the words "the famine was [also] growing more severe in the entire area," and thus the altered text, 41:56-47:1, would read:

> [56] People from all over the area came to Egypt to obtain rations from Joseph, since the famine was [also] growing severe in the entire area. [1] Because of the famine in Canaan, when Jacob learned that there were provisions in Egypt, he said to his sons, "Why are you fantasizing?"

Left where they appear, the words "because of the famine in Canaan" seem anti-climactic. Moved, they seem redundant. Thus, what purpose they serve is not clear.

When the brothers, having journeyed to Egypt, stand before Joseph, it is not clear why the text asserts twice, in 42:7-8, that he recognizes them.

> [7] Joseph recognized his brothers as soon as he saw them. But he behaved like a stranger and spoke harshly to them. "Where are you from?" he asked. "From the land of Canaan—to buy food," they replied. [8] Joseph recognized his brothers, but they did not recognize him.

Why "Joseph recognized his brothers" should not be removed either from 42:7 or 42:8 is not clear.

Nor is the dialogue about spying that unfolds clear; because it is not clear why Joseph charges the brothers with spying, or why they undermine their plausible defense by repeatedly offering more information than is asked for, and fail to note that Joseph reiterates, but does not support, his charge, and that satisfying his seemingly irrelevant demands will not exonerate them. Nor is it clear why they think they are in terrible trouble, or that the trouble is their punishment for having murdered Joseph, whom they last saw, years earlier, alive.

As will be seen, Joseph's pretense for charging, in 42:9, the brothers are spies is, according to Midrash, that they entered the Egyptian city in which food was sold in a suspicious manner, and spent three days in a disreputable neighborhood. In fact, he levels the charge because "he remembered what he had dreamed about them." But the cause and effect are not clear. As noted, he dreamed they would bow down to him. But why that memory, and its seeming actualization—in 42:5, "When Joseph's brothers arrived, they prostrated themselves to him, with their faces to the ground"—should prompt the charge is not clear; if, indeed, they do prompt the charge. As will be seen, it is not clear that the memory has been actualized. And even if it has been, it is not clear that Joseph therefore decides the time has come for his entire family to be settled in Egypt. Nor, even if he has decided that, is it clear how his intent will be furthered by charging that the brothers are spies, because Joseph cannot know, when he levels the charge, that it will prompt the brothers to talk about Benjamin, and thus set in motion the elaborate charade that will reunite the family in Egypt.

Because the brothers appear before Joseph, in 42:5, together, their defense—that they have appeared openly for the innocent purpose of buying food—is plausible. But they undermine it by saying more than they should.

Their tendency to do so (which, as will be seen, many traditionalists argue, for the most part obliquely, is only apparent) appears in 42:7, and persists, to dangerous effect. In their response to Joseph's first question, "Where are you from?" they say that they are from Canaan; and add, unasked, that they have come "to buy food." The charge of spying against them repeated, in 42:11, they say, once again unasked, that they are "all the sons of the same man"; and repeat again, in 42:13, that they are "the sons of one man who is in Canaan," and that "the youngest brother is with our father, and one brother is gone."

It does not occur to the brothers that the proof Joseph demands of their innocence will prove nothing. One of them, he asserts in 42:16, is to return to Canaan, and bring Benjamin to Egypt. "This will test your claim and determine if you are telling the truth. If not, by Pharaoh's life, you will be considered spies." But how the appearance of Benjamin will prove they are not spies is not clear, because the two matters seem entirely unrelated. If he appears, Joseph will presumably acknowledge that he is their younger brother. But why he will therefore conclude they are not spies is not clear.

Nor is it clear why Joseph changes the conditions related to the test: why he asserts, in 42:16, that nine of them will remain imprisoned until the tenth returns with Benjamin, but three days later asserts, in 42:18, that only one of them will remain imprisoned, until the other nine return with Benjamin.

That the brothers should regard their predicament as punishment for the sin they committed against Joseph is understandable. But it is not clear why they regard the predicament as dire; why they seem convinced they murdered Joseph; or why Joseph, overhearing their conversation, weeps.

That conscience should afflict them in 42:21 is not difficult to understand. And Joseph does seem to threaten them with death, when he asserts in 42:20 that, if they return with Benjamin, "you will not die." But because, to placate him, they must do nothing more than return with Benjamin, it is not clear why they seem convinced, in 42:22, that a "great misfortune" has come upon them. Nor is it clear why they seem to agree with Reuben, in 42:22, that "an accounting is being demanded for [Joseph's] blood," because, as noted, they have no reason to believe that Joseph is dead. And why Joseph cries is not clear.

Finally, the reaction of the brothers to a discovery they make at an inn on their way home to Canaan is difficult to understand. Having opened his sack to feed his donkey, one of them, in 42:27, sees his money, and exclaims, in 42:28, that it "has been returned . . . . It's in my sack!" The other brothers seem profoundly shaken.

> Their hearts sank. "What is this that God has done to us?" they asked each other with trembling voices.

It is not clear why each of them does not immediately search his sack (especially because each must feed his donkey); why they complete the journey home, report at length to Jacob what has happened, and only then, in 42:35, open their sacks, and discover that the money of each has been returned. It is not clear why—to say nothing of the terror they feel—not even curiosity prompts each of them to open his sack at the inn, or during the days—perhaps the many days—they are on the road home.

(Nor is it clear why, when they return to Egypt with Benjamin, they tell Joseph's overseer, in 43:21, that at the inn "we opened our packs, and each man's money was at the top of his pack.")

According to Ramban, Joseph tends the family's flocks with the sons of Bilhah and Zilpah only. According to Abarbanel, all of his brothers merely supervise shepherds tending the flocks, and Joseph supervises all of his brothers. According to Sforno, Joseph instructs all of his brothers in shepherding. According to Rashi, Joseph tends the flock together with all of his brothers. Radak agrees; and adds that, because he is inexperienced, the brothers instruct him in shepherding. According to Daat Mikrah, the sons of Bilhah and Zilpah instruct him in shepherding. According to Rashbam and Chizkuni, Joseph tends the flock with the sons of Leah only. According to Malbim, Joseph shepherds his brothers spiritually—he instructs them in virtue—while they shepherd the flock.

According to Rashi, after his age is given as seventeen, Joseph is called "a lad" (*naar*) to indicate he is vain of his appearance, because he is immature. According to Ibn Ezra, because he is a *naar*, he is exploited by the sons of Bilhah and Zilpah, who make him their servant. According to Alshich, because he is a *naar* he serves them as a matter of course (not, apparently, because they exploit him). According to Abarbanel, *naar* is a compliment: though he is only a lad, he is in charge of all of the shepherding, because, as noted, he supervises all of his brothers. According to Rashbam, the words "and he was a lad (*naar*) with the sons of his father's wives Bilhah and Zilpah" indicate that he acts immaturely primarily when he consorts with the sons of Bilhah and Zilpah. According to Daat Mikrah, the same words indicate that Jacob instructs the sons of Bilhah and Zilpah to educate Joseph. According to Sforno, *naar* indicates that, because he is immature, Joseph sins against his brothers by bringing bad reports about them to their father. According to Malbim, Joseph serves his brothers because he thinks it is appropriate that, as a *naar*, he do so. According to Ramban, he is called *naar* because he is less robust physically than his brothers, and because he is the youngest of the brothers involved in shepherding. (Ramban apparently assumes that Benjamin does not participate in the shepherding.)

According to Rashi, Ramban, and Malbim, the opening words of 37:2—"These are the chronicles of Jacob"—begin the narrative that occupies the rest of Genesis; in effect, the chronicles of the lives of Jacob's children. Rashbam, who agrees, explains why the words cannot be understood as introducing a list of the progeny of Jacob (that is, why 37:2 cannot be parallel in meaning to 36:1, which introduces the chronicles of Esau). According to Ibn Ezra, Radak, and Sforno, the words refer to the events that occur to Jacob. According to Chizkuni, the words "These are the chronicles of Jacob, Joseph" indicate that the story of Joseph, interrupted by the chronicles of Esau, is resuming. Or Hachayim offers as the plain meaning of the words an interpretation Rashi seems to regard as homiletic: the assertion, in Midrash Rabbah 84:3, that because Jacob wishes to live in tranquility, a luxury God typically refuses to grant to saintly men, the anguish of Joseph's disappearance is inflicted upon him. (Or Hachayim offers two other possibilities as the plain meaning of the words.) According to Abarbanel, because only Joseph emulates Jacob's virtues, only he can properly be called his progeny, and thus only his life deserves to be chronicled.

According to Malbim, Joseph does not bring to his father any bad report—any slander—of his own regarding any of his brothers; he reports the evil rumors the sons of Leah are spreading about the sons of Bilhah and Zilpah, and those the sons of Bilhah and Zilpah are spreading about the sons of Leah. And he does so in the pious hope that his father will admonish them. According to Sforno, the bad report is that the brothers are neglecting their work as shepherds. According to Rashi and Or Hachayim, who reference Bereshit Rabbah 84:7, Joseph brings to his father a bad report about the sons of Leah only: that they eat the limbs of living animals, demean the sons of Bilhah and Zilpah, and engage in illicit sexual relationships. According to Rashbam, Joseph tells his father that, unlike Leah's sons, he treats the sons of Bilhah and Zilpah with respect. According to Ibn Ezra, Joseph complains to his father that the sons of Bilhah and Zilpah have made him their servant. According to Ramban, he slanders only the sons of Bilhah and Zilpah; and in a particularly nasty fashion, as the seeming redundancy of *dibatam ra* ("a bad report") indicates. According to Radak, Joseph tells his father his brothers hate him. According to Daat Mikrah and Alshich, the words "Joseph brings (*va'yavei*) his father (*el avihem*) a bad report about them" compliment Joseph, because the use of "brought" rather than "disseminated" (*va'yotza*) shows his restraint, as does the fact that he brings the report only to his father. According to Abarbanel and Alshich, Joseph repeats to his father—and only to his father—slander about his brothers that he hears in the marketplace, but that he himself does not believe.

According to Ababanel and Kli Yakar, Jacob loves Joseph more than he loves his other sons because Joseph is superior to them in wisdom, as he shows in the diversity of his responses: by behaving, for example, as a *naar*, a youth, when consorting with the sons of Bilhah and Zilpah, but as a *ben z'kunim*—not "a child of his old age," but "a wise son who understands the deference due to old age"—when consorting with his old and saintly father. According to Rashi, *ben z'kunim* may be taken literally; or the words may mean that Joseph is preeminent in wisdom; or *z'kunim* is a play on two Aramaic words that assert that Joseph's facial features are identical to Jacob's. According to Ibn Ezra, the words must be taken literally, and they apply to Benjamin as well as to Joseph. Rashbam agrees that they must be taken literally; but adds that Joseph is the last of Jacob's eleven children born in Padan-Aram, and that Benjamin is not born until many years after *ben z'kunim* is asserted. According to Radak, the words cannot be taken literally, because all of Jacob's sons are born within seven years; they mean that Joseph is preeminent in wisdom. According to Ramban, Joseph cannot be singled out as literally a *ben z'kunim*, because all of Jacob's sons are born to him in his old age, and because, as noted, Issachar and Zebulun are about the same age as Joseph; and the words *ben z'kunim* mean Joseph attends Jacob in his old age. According to Siftei Chachamim, all of Jacob's sons except Benjamin are born within six years; people become accustomed to calling the youngest of them, Joseph, *ben z'kunim*; and continue to do so when Benjamin is born, years later. According to Chizkuni, Jacob does not love Benjamin, who is indeed younger than Joseph, as much as he loves Joseph, because Rachel died giving birth to Benjamin. According to Malbim, Jacob loves Joseph especially either because *ben z'kunim* is intended literally, or because Joseph attends him in his old age.

About why, in 37:8, Joseph's brothers hate him for "his words" as well as for relating his dream, and about why a single dream is referred to as "dreams," in the plural, opinions differ.

According to Rashi, Ralbag, and Rashbam, "his words" refer to the bad report—the slander of the brothers—that Joseph brings to their father. According to Rabbenu Bachya, Sforno, and Ramban, they refer to Joseph's seeming arrogance in instructing the brothers, in 37:4, to "Listen to the dream I had." (Rabbenu Bachya also notes his three-fold repetition in 37:7 of "behold!"—*v'hinei*—which Kaplan does not translate.) According to Kli Yakar, Joseph does not instruct his brothers arrogantly, but petitions them humbly, to listen to his dream; but they are so incensed by its substance that, despite their resolve not to talk to Joseph at all, they blurt out an indignant response, and hate Joseph the more that "his words" have provoked it. According to Or Hachayim, the brothers object both to Joseph's assertion that he has had a dream ("his dreams"), and to the fact that he recounts it ("his words"). According to Malbim, their hatred increases because they are convinced that "his dreams" reflect what he has been thinking during his waking hours, and "his words" prove that he wants to be appointed their ruler at once.

According to Or Hachayim, although 37:8 speaks of only one dream, the plural is used because each of the three times Joseph says "behold!"—*v'hinei*—the brothers assume Joseph is speaking about a different dream; therefore they think that he recounts three dreams. According to Sforno and Alshich, "dreams" denotes the particulars of a single dream. According to Meam Loez, in 37:5 Joseph has a dream that he does not recount, and another dream, in 37:6-8, that he does recount; and thus "dreams" is to be understood literally.

According to Rashi, Jacob rebukes Joseph in 37:10 for seeming to predict that his mother, Rachel, who is dead, will one day bow down to him.

Unaware that Joseph is referring to Bilhah, who raised him, Jacob undermines the credibility of the dream in order to nullify the brothers' jealousy. Ralbag and Or Hachayim agree that that is why he undermines it. Whether Rashi and Ralbag think Jacob regards all of the dream as prophetic is not clear; according to Or Hachayim, Sforno, and Siftei Chachamim, Jacob does. According to Rashbam, Jacob would have rebuked Joseph for the reference to Rachel even if she had still been alive. Ibn Ezra agrees that Joseph is referring to Bilhah. According to Ramban, Jacob's assumption that the moon in 37:9 in Joseph's second dream—"The sun, the moon, and eleven stars were bowing down to me"—refers to any of his wives is mistaken; it refers, in his opinion, to all of his descendants who go down to Egypt, except Joseph's brothers ("the eleven stars"). According to Rabbenu Bachya, on the one hand, because Rachel could not bow down to Joseph, Jacob discounts the entire dream; on the other hand, he thinks it prophetic and looks forward to its fulfillment.

According to Rabbenu Bachya, commenting on 37:11, though the usual cause of hatred is jealousy, and the brothers already hate Joseph at 37:4, because of the colorful coat, they do not become jealous in earnest until 34:11, when they begin to take seriously the possibility that his dreams are prophetic, and that in consequence he may end up dominating them. (Why they do hate him Rabbenu Bachya does not seem to say; not, it seems, because of the colorful coat, which, he says, rouses only glancing jealousy.) According to Radak, commenting on 37:3, the brothers begin to hate Joseph because they are jealous of the colorful coat, and enraged that Joseph has slandered them. According to Ramban, commenting on 37:4, the sons of Bilhah and Zilpah hate Joseph because of their jealousy. According to Malbim, the brothers' jealousy begins at 37:11, when they realize that Joseph's dreams may be prophetic, and that therefore he may end up dominating them. According to Alshich, the brothers hate Joseph at 37:4 not because of jealousy, but because they fear that Jacob loves Joseph more than he loves them, and that therefore he will believe the slander about them that Joseph reports to him. According to Or Hachayim and Ralbag, commenting on 37:3, the brothers begin to hate Joseph in 37:4 because they cannot bear the combined pressure of two facts: that Joseph slanders them to Jacob, and that, through the colorful coat, Jacob in effect asserts publicly that he loves Joseph more than he loves them. And they are jealous of Joseph in 37:11 because they think God may have spoken to him in the dreams. According to Daat Mikrah, the sons of Leah begin to hate Joseph in 37:4 because of jealousy, and the sons of Bilhah and Zilpah begin to hate him because he slanders them to Jacob. According to Sforno, the brothers envy Joseph in 37:11 because Jacob loves him so deeply, he will listen to anything he recounts, even a seemingly arrogant dream. According to Abarbanel, the brothers begin to hate Joseph in 37:2, when they begin to suspect that he has slandered them to Jacob; and they stop hating him in 37:11, because they stop suspecting that he has slandered them, and begin to be jealous of him, because they begin to suspect that God may have spoken to him in the dreams. According to Meam Loez and Daat Mikrah, the brothers' jealousy in 37:11 compounds their hatred.

Because, given the diversity of opinions above, it is not possible to establish why the brothers become jealous in 37:11, and because, as noted, the second of the two assertions in 37:11—"his father suspended judgment"—is cryptic or vague, the meaning of the verse is not clear. In Kaplan's translation, it is not clear what matter Jacob is thinking about, and suspends judgment about, the brothers' jealousy, or Joseph's second dream (or both). In fact, it is not clear what "suspended judgment" means. And Kaplan's translation is misleading, because the second assertion, translated literally, reads (as Kaplan notes), "his father kept the matter in mind." But that translation is vague, because it does not specify what matter Jacob keeps in mind, or what his thoughts about the matter are. Traditionalists seem to agree that Jacob is thinking about Joseph's dream. About what he is thinking, however, they differ. According to Rashi and Sforno, Jacob looks forward to the fulfillment of the prophesy in Joseph's dream. According to Rashbam, when the brothers inform him, in 45:25, that Joseph is alive, and viceroy in Egypt, he believes them, because through the twenty-two years of Joseph's absence he has kept in mind the prophesy in the dream. According to Or Hachayim, Jacob does not believe his own dismissive commentary on the dream that he hopes will placate the brothers: that because it is impossible that he and his dead wife will bow down to Joseph, the dream cannot be prophetic. According to Radak, Jacob keeps the dream in mind, but is not sure what it means. According to Ralbag, Jacob is immediately sure the dream is prophetic.

According to Abarbanel, the seeming wordiness of 37:12-14 underscores Jacob's desire not to favor Joseph, and Joseph's desire to obey his father. Jacob thinks it unfair that Joseph should sit comfortably at home while his brothers are shepherding at Shechem, and therefore suggests (but does not order) that Joseph join them. Joseph consents immediately, because he is humbly zealous to serve his father. According to Rashi, he consents though he knows his brothers hate him (and, presumably, may therefore try to harm him). According to Meam Loez, because Jacob knows that the brothers hate Joseph and are jealous of him, that to reach them he must cross dangerous open country, that Shechem itself is dangerous, and that a servant could easily make the trip, his recklessness in sending Joseph must demonstrate that God is using him to institute his descent, together with his progeny, into Egypt. Malbim agrees. According to Rashbam, Shechem is dangerous because its inhabitants must remember that in 34:25-27 two of the brothers plundered the city in retaliation for the rape of their sister Dina. According to Radak, Jacob does not think the journey will endanger Joseph; and Joseph is not afraid his brothers will try to harm him, because he is convinced that their hatred of him will be governed by their fear of their father. According to Daat Mikrah, Joseph humbly and eagerly obeys his father, though he knows his brothers hate him (and presumably, therefore, may try to harm him). According to Or Hachayim, Jacob believes that Joseph will be protected from the hatred of his brothers because he is honoring his father by obeying his order to visit them. According to Ralbag, Jacob sends Joseph to Shechem though he understands its inhabitants are furious that the two brothers plundered their city, and may therefore harm him. (Why Jacob would expose him to such harm Ralbag does not say.) According to Alshich, Jacob knows Joseph may be harmed by the inhabitants of Shechem, or by his brothers, and therefore does not order him to undertake the journey until he decides, on his own, to undertake it. According to Abarbanel, Jacob never suspects the brothers intend to harm Joseph.

According to Rashi, Abarbanel, and Or Hachayim, the man Joseph meets in the field is an angel; according to Rashi and Abarbanel, the angel Gabriel. According to Or Hachayim, Joseph does not realize the man is an angel. According to Alshich and Ramban, referencing Bereshit Rabbah 84:13, which notes that "a man" is repeated three times, Joseph meets three angels, Gabriel, Michael, and Raphael, each bearing a different message. According to Ibn Ezra, Joseph meets a man passing by.

According to Gur Aryeh, whose position is paraphrased in Siftei Chachomim, though the entire episode in the field seems unnecessary, it indicates that God, acting through an angel, is instituting the process by which Jacob and his progeny will be drawn down to Egypt; otherwise, having failed to locate his brothers in Shechem, Joseph would not have blundered about, but would have returned home. According to Ramban and

Rashbam, the words "blundering about in the fields" bespeak many unspecified difficulties that prompt Joseph to return home that he disregards in order to honor his father's order. According to Alshich, "blundering" indicates that, as the first angel tells Joseph, he has partially misinterpreted the first of his dreams.

According to Abarbanel, the hidden meaning in the man's question to Joseph—"What are you looking for?"—is that the brothers will try to harm him; a meaning Joseph does not understand. According to Alshich, the man—in fact, the second angel—is asking Joseph whether he wants peace with his brothers, or strife. And his answer—"I'm looking for my brothers"—means that, whatever they want, he wants peace. According to Ralbag, the question, and the subsequent exchanges, seem to have only their apparent meanings. According to Rashi, beneath the plain meanings in the man's last two assertions—that the brothers have already "left this area," and that he has "heard them planning to go to Dothan"—are hidden meanings: respectively, that the brothers no longer feel related to Joseph, and that they are planning to kill him. According to Malbim, the closing assertion should have made Joseph suspicious; because Dothan is so far from Shechem, it should have occurred to him that the brothers want to lure him far from home, then to kill him. According to Alshich, the third angel tells Joseph that his brothers have gone to Dothan; that is, that they have distanced themselves completely from him.

As noted, Reuben and Judah are not among the would-be murderers. According to Daat Mikrah, Simon wants to put an arrow through Joseph at a distance. According to Meam Loez, who references Targum Yonatan, the chief conspirators are Simon and Levi. Abarbanel agrees, fixing on them by a process of elimination, and noting that the blood-thirst that prompted them to slaughter all the men in Shechem to avenge the rape of Dina prompts them to kill Joseph in Shechem. According to Ralbag, the brothers conspire equally.

Perhaps because the ease with which Reuben convinces the other brothers not to murder Joseph strains credibility, traditionalists assert that Reuben proposes—as a ploy, because he plans to rescue Joseph—only that Joseph be murdered indirectly, and that the other brothers agree only to that proposal. But they differ about how Reuben advances his proposal. It is not clear what, in Reuben's opinion, the immediate consequences of the proposal will be.

According to Rashbam, Ralbag, Rabbenu Bachya, Ramban, and Sforno, Reuben tricks the brothers into casting Joseph into a deep well (from which he hopes to rescue him). According to Rashbam, Malbim and Ralbag, he convinces the brothers that Joseph will die by himself if they merely cast him into a well; and in the desert, where the chance that people will pass by and rescue him is slight. According to Ralbag, Rabbenu Bachya, Ramban, and Sforno, he convinces them also not actually to spill blood.

According to Rashi, referencing Shabbat 72a, and commenting on the assertion in 37:25 that the well into which the brothers throw Joseph "was empty; there was no water in it," the well does contain poisonous snakes and scorpions. Ramban disagrees; in his opinion, the seemingly unnecessary words "there was no water in it" simply underscore that the well is completely dry. The disagreement is material to the discussion of Reuben's intent, because, if the well does contain poisonous snakes and scorpions, and Reuben knows it, he must realize that his proposal exposes Joseph to mortal danger, and therefore, it seems, his intention cannot be to rescue him from the brothers. Thus, it seems, Reuben must think that the well is empty. But according to Alshich, referencing The Zohar, Reuben sees the snakes and scorpions, and nonetheless advances his proposal, because he is certain that they will be awed intuitively by the saintliness of Joseph, and will not in consequence harm him. (The Zohar does not seem to share Alshich's certainty, because it assigns to Reuben only the hope that the snakes and scorpions will not harm Joseph.) According to Ramban, even if the Talmud that Rashi references is correct, it must be that Reuben does not see the snakes and scorpions, because they live in cracks in the well, or because the well is very deep; because if he did see them, he would understand the mortal danger they pose to Joseph, and withdraw his proposal.

According to Rashi, Reuben rescues Joseph because he thinks that, because he is the eldest of the brothers, Jacob will blame only him for Joseph's death. According to Meam Loez, either of two motives may prompt Reuben: he thinks that, if the other brothers do kill Joseph and later regret having done so, they will rebuke him for not having stopped them; or he is grateful that, though in 35:21 he apparently violated his stepmother Bilhah, Joseph still regards him as a brother, because in his second dream eleven brothers (including Reuben) bow down to him. According to Abarbanel and Daat Mikrah, Reuben saves Joseph as penance for the sin he committed against Bilhah.

Because when the Ishmaelites appear all of the brothers, including Judah, still seem resolved to kill Joseph—though not directly, by shedding his blood—it is not clear why Judah suddenly suggests he be sold instead, and why the other brothers agree. Neither matter seems to have prompted commentary. And a few commentaries that seem to hint at an impulse of conscience in Judah, and perhaps in the other brothers, are especially puzzling, because Judah's assertion in 37:26 that they will gain nothing if "we kill our brother and cover his blood" in essence reiterates Reuben's proposal—that the other brothers seem not to regard as a ploy, and that does not seem related in their minds to conscience—that they kill Joseph, though without actually bloodying their hands. Thus, for example, the assertion of Alshich that Judah decides Joseph should not die when he realizes he must be saintly, because the snakes and the scorpions in the well, he notices, do not injure him, and the assertions of Sforno and Meam Loez that Judah realizes conscience will torment him and his brothers if they kill Joseph— an assertion which the other brothers seem to take seriously, because they agree that Joseph be sold—is inconsistent with the unshaken resolve of all the brothers, including Judah, to kill Joseph.

According to Rashi, commenting on 37:28, Joseph is sold several times. The brothers pull him from the well, and sell him to a caravan of Ishmaelites, who then sell him to a caravan of Midianites, who carry him to Egypt and sell him to Egyptians. According to Ramban, from a distance the caravan approaching seems to the brothers to be of Ishmaelites; but it turns out to be a caravan of Midianites under contract to Ishmaelites. The Midianites buy Joseph from the brothers, who pull him from the well, and turn him over to the Ishmaelites, who sell him into slavery in Egypt. According to Rashbam, Rabbenu Bachya, and Malbim, the caravan of Midianites arrives at the well before the caravan of Ishmaelites does. The Midianites pull Joseph out of the well, and sell him to the Ishmaelites. The brothers are unaware of the sale. The Ishmaelites, sometimes, as in 37:36, called Midanites, then sell Joseph into slavery in Egypt. (Whether Malbim agrees that the brothers are unaware of the sale is not clear.) According to Bereshit Rabbah 84:22, the Ishmaelites, Midianites, and Midanites are separate groups of Arabs. According to Ibn Ezra, only one caravan, first called Ishmaelite and then Midianite, passes by. Its merchants pull Joseph from the well. According to Ralbag, the brothers pull Joseph from the well, and sell him to the merchants of the caravan, who are called, variously, Ishmaelites, Midianites, and Midanites. According to Sforno, the Ishmaelites are driving the caravan for its owners, the Midianites. The brothers negotiate with the Ishmaelites. But the Midianites (sometimes known as Midanites) pull Joseph out of the well, and sell him into slavery in Egypt. According to Or Hachayim, the brothers sell Joseph to the Ishmaelites. The Midianites broker that sale, as well as the sale of Joseph into slavery in Egypt. According to Radak, the Ishmaelites, the Midianites, and the Midanites are the same people. According to Kli Yakar, the brothers sell Joseph to the Ishmaelites, who will, they hope, treat him mercifully, because they are descended from Abraham. They, however, resell him quickly, at a profit, to the Midianites, without the consent, or, indeed, the knowledge, of the brothers. And the Midianites (sometimes called Midanites) sell Joseph into slavery in Egypt. According to Alshich, the Midianites do not participate in any way in the sale of Joseph; they are mentioned only to underscore that the brothers insist on selling him only to Ishmaelites, because they are on their way to Egypt, and the brothers are convinced the Egyptians will enslave Joseph forever. According to Abarbanel, the merchants in the caravan that passes are Midianites, a sub-group of Ishmaelites.

Abarbanel, Ralbag, and Malbim, commenting on 37:29, note that Reuben is not present when the other brothers sell Joseph, but do not explain why. According to Rashi, he is either taking his turn caring for Jacob, a task the brothers share, or doing penance for having violated Bilhah. According to Meam Loez, he is doing penance, though he did not violate her, but merely moved her bed. According to Siftei Chachamim, he is doing penance in private, his preparation for public confession. According to Daat Mikrah, he is busy tending the family's sheep.

According to Malbim, the verb that opens 42:1, *va'yar*, indicates that Jacob literally sees merchants returning from Egypt with food, and therefore instructs his sons to journey to Egypt. According to Daat Mikrah, *va'yar* can convey Malbim's meaning, or it can mean Jacob "hears and understands." According to Rashi, who plays on the word *shever*, the use of *va'yar* in 42:1 indicates that Jacob is granted an indistinct prophetic hint that hope [*shever*] resides in Egypt, and the first verb in 42:2, *shamati*, indicates he also hears that food [*shever*] is available in Egypt. According to Ibn Ezra, Chizkuni, Ralbag, and Saadia Gaon, *va'yar* has the same meaning as *shamati*. Thus, in 42:1 Jacob hears that food is available in Egypt, and in 42:2 tells his sons what he heard. According to Radak, Jacob sees (*va'yar*) merchants returning from Egypt, and then hears (*shamati*) from them what they bought there. According to Rabbenu Bachya, *va'yar* indicates spiritual insight as well as mundane understanding.

According to Malbim, Jacob rebukes the brothers in *titra'u*, which he translates as "to be looked upon," which indicates he is censuring them for being looked upon as indifferent to their poverty, when they can do as the merchants did. According to Sforno, *titra'u* indicates the brothers are looking ineffectually at one another, each waiting to hear a course of action suggested. According to Ramban, *titra'u* is part of a rhetorical question—"Why are you showing your faces here?"—which asserts, in effect, that they should be on their way to Egypt. According to Rashi, *titra'u* can mean that, to mislead the Ishmaelites, the brothers are pretending they still have enough food; that they are encouraging others to look at them and wonder why they are not taking effective action before they run out of food; or that they are becoming lean through hunger. According to Rashbam and Ibn Ezra, they are showing off, pretending to their neighbors that they have enough food. According to Ibn Ezra, Jacob is encouraging them to look one another in the face—that is to say, not to quarrel. According to Saadia Gaon, *titra'u* means that the brothers have become weak. According to Meam Loez, Jacob is worried that the Ishmaelites, passing through Canaan on their way to Egypt, will be convinced by the brothers' charade that they have plenty of food, and will demand that they feed them; or he cautions his sons not "to show themselves" in Canaan, where they want to search for food, lest they be attacked because two of them wiped out Shechem. According to Radak, Jacob asks why the brothers are sitting at home, pretending to have enough food, when everyone else is off buying food.

According to Malbim, and Alshich, the seeming repetition in 42:5 of the fact that a famine exists underscores that the charge the brothers are spies is baseless; like the many others among whom they appear, they have been drawn to Egypt by hunger. According to Or Hachayim, the repetition indicates a clever ruse devised by the brothers: they appear among the others ostensibly because of the famine, but in fact because they have come to Egypt to search for Joseph. (According to Rabbenu Bachya, referencing Midrash Rabbah 91:6, they spend three days searching for him in brothels, thinking that, because he is handsome, they may find him among prostitutes.)

According to Ibn Ezra, Meam Loez, and Sforno, in 42:7 Joseph recognizes his brothers as a group, whereas in 42:8 he recognizes them individually. According to Alshich and Ramban, in 42:7 Joseph thinks that they are his brothers; but only after they say they have come from Canaan is he certain; and so only then does the text repeat, in 42:8, that he recognizes them. According to Malbim and Abarbanel, in 42:7 he recognizes them by their faces; but only after he hears them speak is he certain who they are.

According to Baal Haturim, in 42:7 Joseph recognizes his brothers at once; but so does the angel Gabriel, the "man" who met Joseph wandering in the field in 37:15, and who, standing invisibly at Joseph's side, reminds him of the brothers' cruelty. By contrast, in 42:8, the angel is gone, and only Joseph recognizes his brothers.

According to Midrash, referenced by Rabbenu Bachya, each of the brothers, acting on instructions from Jacob, enters the city in which food is being sold through a different gate. A functionary records the name of each as he enters. When Joseph finds the names of all the brothers in the records, he orders all the storehouses but one closed, and waits for the brothers, who have reassembled, to arrive there. When three days have passed and they have not arrived, he has them rounded up and brought to him. They have spent the three days searching for him in a neighborhood filled with brothels, for the reason noted.

Many traditionalists reference the Midrash above to explain why Joseph charges that the brothers are spies. As noted, however, because their seemingly suspicious and disreputable behavior is merely Joseph's pretense for advancing the charge, why he does advance it cannot be clarified by reference to the Midrash.

Nor, it seems, can the matter be clarified by reference to Joseph's dreams regarding the brothers, because it is not clear what Joseph is thinking when he remembers the dreams, and because, as noted, the relevance of whatever he is thinking to the charge the brothers are spies is not clear; if, indeed, what he is thinking is relevant.

According to Rashi, Joseph thinks the first of his dreams has been actualized, because the brothers have bowed down to him; and therefore, Rashi perhaps presumes, he decides his family should come to Egypt. But Rashi does not say that he presumes that. Ramban does not presume it. He thinks that, in Joseph's opinion, the dream has not been actualized, because Benjamin has not bowed down to him. And he does not explain why Joseph does assert the brothers are spies. He does not say it is because Joseph remembers his dreams. And he does not reference the Midrash. (He does in his commentary on 42:11.) Perhaps, he says, the brothers rouse suspicions because they are the first Canaanites to come to buy food.

According to Or Hachayim, Joseph levels a charge at the brothers that he knows is not true because he remembers, when he recalls his dreams, that they accused him of interpreting it in an untrue fashion.

According to Malbim, because people under interrogation rouse suspicion if they answer questions not asked, in 42:7 the brothers begin to undermine their plausible defense by telling Joseph that they have come to Egypt "to buy food" when he asks only where they have come from. But in Malbim's opinion, as in that of other traditionalists who consider the dialogue between Joseph and the brothers, they do not thereafter offer more information than they should.

According to Malbim, their assertion in 42:10 that they are "all sons of the same man" argues, in effect, that no single family would send as many as ten spies. Their assertion that they "would never think of being spies" argues, in effect, that they have never been professional spies. (Sforno and Rabbenu Bachya agree.) And their response, in 42:13, to Joseph's charge in 42:12 that they have "come to see where the land is exposed" argues, in effect, that they cannot be spies, because it is inconceivable that their father would have exposed virtually all of his children to the dangers of spying. Ralbag agrees.

According to Ramban, the brothers assert they are "all sons of the same man" to underscore either that Jacob sent them together because they did not want to be separated, or that their father is an eminent and righteous person; or to protect from theft the food they would buy.

According to Or Hachayim and Sforno, the brothers assert, in effect, that it would make no sense to send as spies ten members of the same family.

According to Rashbam, Radak, and Rabbenu Bachya, the brothers argue they have come together because they are all sons of the same man.

According to Rashi, the brothers offer the information in 42:13 to underscore that they have come to Egypt to search for their lost brother.

According to Or Hachayim, in his commentary on Joseph's assertion in 42:15—"There is only one way you can convince me" the charge of spying is unfounded—Joseph agrees to accept the explanation Benjamin presumably will offer of why the brothers came to Egypt; though why he should do so, and therefore accept that they are not spies, is, Or Hachayim admits, not clear.

According to Sforno, the appearance of Benjamin will prove that he is indeed one of the brothers. (How that will convince Joseph the brothers are not spies Sforno does not say.)

According to Siftei Chachamim, if Benjamin does not appear, Joseph will conclude the brothers are beyond question spies; if he does appear, he will continue to doubt whether or not they are. (Thus, in the opinion of Siftei Chachamim, Benjamin's appearance will prove nothing.)

According to Alshich, when Benjamin appears, he will be subjected to severe punishment; and, being young and therefore unable to endure it, he will reveal whether or not the brothers are spies. (Why Joseph will assume Benjamin knows whether or not the brothers are spies Alshich does not say.)

According to Abarbanel, two interpretations of "There is only one way you can convince me" are plausible. Either Joseph will interrogate Benjamin, in the expectation that, being young and guileless, he will discuss honestly whether or not the brothers are spies; or "There is only one way you can convince me" refers not to Benjamin, but to the brothers, who will for the first time be rigorously interrogated. In this second interpretation, Abarbanel asserts that interrogating Benjamin would prove nothing—literally, that it would not constitute a test at all (*ki lo ha'yah b'zeh bechinah chlal*). But what he means by that is not clear.

According to Or Hachayim, Joseph is forced in 42:18 to revise the test he proposes in 42:16 because the brothers reject the first proposal, out of concern for their father, or because they refuse to be separated. They are concerned that their father will worry about the fate of the brothers still imprisoned, and that, remembering Joseph was lost on a journey, will not permit Benjamin to go to Egypt. They agree, after three days of imprisonment, to the revised proposal because it is their only means of proving that they are not spies.

According to Daat Mikrah, during the three days of imprisonment the brothers resolve unanimously to reject Joseph's first proposal, and therefore Joseph is forced to offer a second, less onerous, proposal. (Why they resolve to reject the first one Daat Mikrah does not say.)

According to Kli Yakar, when at first Joseph imprisons all of the brothers, he is certain that they will elect Reuben, the eldest, to return to Canaan, and hopes that they may consider Reuben has earned freedom, because he tried to rescue Joseph from them. After three days, Joseph frees all of them except Simon because he thinks that they have repented of their sin (*a'von*) against him, but remembers that Simon provoked the others to that sin.

According to Malbim, the brothers reject the first proposal because it entails all of them remaining in prison. Because, as Joseph realizes, any of the brothers could recruit any young man to impersonate Benjamin, or could explain to Benjamin, or the recruit, how to corroborate their story, he first proposes that a functionary be sent to Canaan to fetch Benjamin, who will be interrogated before he speaks with his brothers. The brothers reject this proposal because they realize that Jacob would never send Benjamin to Egypt with a functionary. And when Joseph realizes, after three days, that the brothers will continue to reject the proposal, he revises it.

According to Alshich, Joseph's first proposal requires that all of the brothers remain in prison, and that a functionary go for Benjamin. During the three-day period of imprisonment, Joseph realizes that the brothers are terrified that under interrogation Benjamin will recount the episode of the bloodied coat, in which they argued, in effect, that Joseph was dead, an argument that contradicts their assertion (in Midrash) that they have come to Egypt to search for him; and that the contradiction will convince the viceroy that they murdered their brother, and therefore deserve to die. Realizing this, Joseph reassures them, in the revised proposal, that he will not interrogate Benjamin.

According to Abarbanel, it was perhaps customary in Egypt to imprison suspects for three days, to see if evidence against them, or in their behalf, would turn up; and therefore Joseph imprisons all of them for that time. He revises his proposal (during the third day, rather than after three full days have passed) to assure them that if they return with Benjamin they will be regarded as having spoken the truth throughout, and evidence against them will not be considered.

According to Or Hachayim and Malbim, the "great misfortune" the brothers refer to in 42:21 is the necessity of leaving Simon in prison until they return with Benjamin. According to Rashbam, the great misfortune is that they have been imprisoned. According to Kli Yakar, in his commentary on 42:22, the great misfortune is that they will be condemned to death if for some reason Benjamin does not appear before Joseph. According to Abarbanel, the great misfortune is that Joseph believes nothing they say.

According to Sforno, Reuben asserts in 42:22 that "an accounting is being demanded for [Joseph's] blood" because he is convinced that the strain of slave labor in Egypt must have killed Joseph. According to Or Hachayim, the brothers are being called to account either for causing Joseph to be killed, or for endangering his life. According to Malbim, they are being called to account either because they acted too stringently in formally condemning him to death (according to Sforno, in his commentary on 37:18, for slandering them, and thus destroying their reputations), or in consigning him to slavery, an approximation of death. According to Daat Mikrah, 42:22 contains a veiled reference to Exodus 21:16, which asserts that the punishment for kidnapping is death whether or not the victim dies. According to Rashi, the brothers are being called to account for the pain they have inflicted upon Jacob as well as upon Joseph. According to Alshich, Reuben convinces the other brothers that they have not repented for selling Joseph into slavery, and therefore, whether or not he is dead, in some metaphoric sense an accounting is being demanded for his blood.

According to Sforno, Joseph cries in 42:24 because his brothers are distressed (why, Sforno does not say); according to Abarbanel and Radak, because he realizes they repent having sinned against him; according to Rashi and Siftei Chachamim, because he hears they are filled with regret (for what, neither commentator says). According to Alshich, he weeps because he remembers the suffering the brothers' treachery caused him; and according to Daat Mikrah, because he thinks about the suffering his father has been enduring.

According to Ramban, only one of the brothers opens his sack at the inn because only he has a weak donkey that requires fodder. The other brothers feed their donkeys straw, and therefore have no need to open their sacks until they return home. According to Malbim, the money each of the brothers pays is placed in a small pouch inside the sack of each, and the pouch is placed at the top of only one of the sacks, so that only one brother discovers his money. (It is not clear whether, according to Malbim, the other brothers search their sacks.) According to Daat Mikrah, citing 43:21, but not 42:35, it is reasonable to suppose that all the brothers check their sacks. (Why each does not find his money, Daat Mikrah does not say.) According to Radak, Joseph orders the money placed at the top of the sack of one brother, and in the middle of the sacks of the other brothers. As a result, all the brothers search their sacks, but only one finds his money. (Why the brothers empty their sacks only when they arrive home, and not at the inn, Radak does not say.) According to Abarbanel, Radak is correct; except that the money is placed in the various sacks by happenstance (*bemikreh*) by one of Joseph's servants.

To understand the plain meaning of the two episodes involving Joseph discussed above, it is necessary to understand why the history of Joseph begins with the assertion that the chronicles of Jacob are about to be presented, whether Joseph brings to his father any bad report—any slander—regarding his brothers, if he does, which of them he slanders, and why, what the slander is, whether the slander demeans or elevates him, whether the brothers know that he has slandered them, why Jacob loves him more than he loves his other sons, precisely why his brothers hate him, why the text asserts that his dreams infuriate them after he has related only one dream, why Jacob rebukes him for relating the second of his dreams, what the interplay is in the brothers between hatred and jealousy, what the meaning is of Jacob's assertion that he suspends judgment about some unspecified matter, why his instruction that Joseph visit his brothers shepherding in a distant field seems to contain too many words, why Jacob instructs him to visit them, if he does, why it worries Joseph, if it does, why he obeys it, who the man is—or the angel is—or the angels are—he meets in the field, why the meeting occurs, who among his brothers conspire to murder him, whether Reuben offers them an alternative to murder, why the well they throw Joseph into is dangerous, if it is, why Reuben wants to rescue him, why Judah proposes they sell him, why the other brothers, though seemingly intent on murder, agree to sell him, how many times he is sold, by whom and to whom, where Reuben is when he is sold, what precisely prompts Jacob to order his sons to journey to Egypt, whether he rebukes them for not responding to the famine in Canaan, if he does, what the rebuke is, why the brothers journey to Egypt, why it is twice asserted that Joseph recognizes them, why he accuses them of being spies apparently as a consequence of remembering his dreams, what it is about the dreams he remembers that prompts the accusation, why the brothers seem to think the information they provide about their family will prove to the viceroy that they are not spies, why they accept his contention that producing Benjamin will prove that he has accused them unjustly, why, after jailing them for three days, Joseph changes the conditions for testing them, what the great misfortune is that they think has come upon them, why they think that they are being punished for having murdered Joseph, who, as they know, may not be dead, why Joseph cries when he overhears them talking, why all of them do not open their sacks at the inn. But it is not possible to understand these matters.

⸺

When the spoken Revelation at Mount Sinai ends, God issues two commands to Moses, the first, in two parts, related to the Jews, the second related to Moses. The second command is problematic; in part because, when it is issued and fulfilled, a problem related to the first command, present during the Revelation, reappears; and, in far more significant part, because Moses seems to delay fulfilling the second command, in order to perform an action that is puzzling because the plain meaning of a significant number of its details is unclear, as is its aftermath.

Moses is commanded, in 20:19-23, to teach the Jews two laws about proper worship, and, in 21:1-23:33, a wide range of civil laws (21:1-23:33); and then, in 24:1-18, to ascend Mount Sinai, twice, first in the company of Jewish leaders, then alone, to receive from God a document He has written.

The concern relating to the first command—where Moses is located when the second command is issued—reprises the concern relating to where he is located at three earlier moments, before, during, and after the Revelation, and foreshadows the concern regarding where he is located when the second command is issued and fulfilled.

When the Jews have encamped at the base of Mount Sinai, in 19:3 Moses "went up to God," and in 19:7 he is commanded to convey an offer to the Jews. In 19:7, he "came [back]" with the offer. When they accept it, in 19:8 he "brought the people's reply back to God," and in 19:9-13 God commands him to spend two days with the Jews preparing them (though they may not know that) for the Revelation. That command fulfilled, in 19:14 Moses "went down from the mountain," and in 19:14-15 prepares the Jews. On the third day, when the Revelation begins, in 19:20 Moses "climbed up" the mountain. In 19:21 God at once commands him to "go back down," to issue (or to repeat) a warning to the Jews about the mountain; and then, in 19:24, seems to repeat that he is to "go down" to the people, and adds immediately that he is to "come [back] up along with Aaron." In 19:25 he "went down to the people." After the spoken Revelation occurs, in 20:16-17 he speaks with the people, seemingly at the foot of the mountain, and then, in 20:18, "entered the mist where the Divine was [revealed]," presumably (but perhaps, as will be seen, not) on the mountain.

With three exceptions, the ascents and descents of Moses noted are rendered in the Hebrew verbs *la'alot* (to ascend) and *la'redet* (to descend). Moreover, *la'redet* is used three times—in 19:11, 19:18, and 19:20—to render the descent of God onto Mount Sinai, and *la'alot* is used four times—in 19:12, 19:13, 19:23, and 19:24—to stipulate when the Jews may, and may not, ascend the mountain. That being the case, the three exceptions, by deviating from the verbal pattern established by the iteration of *la'alot* and *la'redet* may prompt, if not uncertainty or even confusion, at least uneasiness about where Moses is located. And one instance noted above—the instruction in 19:24—in which *la'redet* and *la'alot* are juxtaposed must, it seems, prompt at least uncertainty.

The first exception prompts the least uneasiness. In 19:7, though *va'yavo moshe* means literally only that, before the spoken Revelation, Moses "came" with God's offer to the Jews, Kaplan's bracketed indication that he "came [back]," presumably from the mountain, is plausible. The second exception, the assertion, in 19:8, again before the spoken Revelation, *va'yashev moshe*, is more ambiguous, because *va'yashev* may be rendered as plausibly by "Moses repeated" as by, in Kaplan's translation, Moses "brought . . . back" to God the Jews' acceptance of His offer. And the third exception, the assertion, in 20:18, that after the spoken Revelation Moses "entered the mist where the Divine was [revealed]," does not, except in dramatic context, bespeak ascent, because *nigash*, rendered accurately by Kaplan, means simply "entered," and because the argument from dramatic context, though otherwise strong, is undermined by the single instance, noted above, of the juxtaposition of *la'alot* and *la'redet*.

"The mist" in 20:18 seems the same as the "thick cloud" in which, in 19:9, God says he will come to Moses during the spoken Revelation (though it may not be, because the *av he'anan*, the "thick cloud," of 19:9 and the *arafel*, "the mist," of 20:18 the "heavy cloud," that covers Mount Sinai in 19:16 as the spoken Revelation begins is almost certainly the same as the *av he'anan*, the "thick cloud," of 19:9 (*anan* being the same noun in both verses). That being the case, the dramatic context argues strongly that in 20:18 Moses "ascends [into]," rather than simply "enters [into]," the mist. But that is so only if it can be shown that Moses is on Mount Sinai when the spoken Revelation occurs. And that cannot be shown, because of the juxtaposition noted. And thus the juxtaposition may convert into at least uncertainty the uneasiness regarding the pattern of Moses' ascents and descents.

As noted, in 19:24, God commands Moses to "Go down (*leich reid*). You can then come [back] up (*v'alita*) along with Aaron." In the Hebrew sentence, the verbal pattern discussed above is underscored by the juxtaposition of *reid* and *v'alita*. But in 19:25 Moses seems to follow only half of the instruction: he "went down (*va'yireid*) to the people." Immediately thereafter, without any indication that he goes back up the mountain, either by himself or with Aaron, the spoken Revelation begins. Thus, it is not clear whether Moses fulfills promptly the second half of the command in 19:24; that is, whether he is on the mountain when the spoken Revelation occurs, or at its base. The impulse to assert that Moses must have fulfilled promptly all of God's command is understandable. And an appeal to a text already cited—God's assertion, in 19:9, that he will appear to Moses in a "thick cloud"—would seem to necessitate that Moses is on the mountain when the spoken Revelation occurs. But against the impulse the fact must be set that the text says nothing about where he is. And 19:9 does not say where—whether on the mountain, or at its base—the thick cloud will be in which God will appear. Moreover—and perhaps most important—as noted, when the spoken Revelation ends, Moses seems to be at the base of the mountain, talking, in 20:15-18, with the Jews. And because there is no evidence that he comes down from the mountain, after hearing the spoken Revelation, to talk with them, it seems reasonable to suppose that he has been at the base of the mountain, with the Jews, continuously since 19:25, when he "went down" to them.

If that is the case—and if in consequence it must be supposed that the thick cloud covers Moses at the base of the mountain, rather than on it—it may be reasonable to suppose as well that when, in 20:18, "Moses entered (*nigash*) the mist where the Divine was [revealed]" he does not ascend, but simply enters; a supposition that, as noted above, reflects more accurately than does the supposition of ascent the plain meaning of *nigash*; and that, as will now be seen, seems to obviate a problem that reappears when God issues the second of His commands to Moses, and that persists when (though he delays doing so) he fulfills it.

The second command, issued at 24:1-2, is as follows:

> [1] [God] said to Moses, "Go up (*alei*) to God along with Aaron, Nadav and Avihu, and seventy of the elders of Israel. All of you must then bow down at a distance. [2] Only Moses shall then approach God. The others may not come close, and the people may not go up with him."

But if *nigash* in 20:18 means "ascend" rather than simply "enter," then in 24:1 *alei* cannot mean "go up," because when Moses receives the second of God's commands he has been on the mountain since 20:18, the last time he ascended it. But as *alei* always seems to mean "go up," it seems that *nigash* in 20:18 must mean simply "enter." But, given the relevant discussion above, "must" seems too strong a word. And thus, unless *alei* means, "go down from the mountain, and then come back up"—an improbability, to say the least—it is not possible to know what it does mean in 24:1.

The problem persists when the second command is fulfilled, in God's command related to Moses' descent and ascent.

When, in 24:3,"Moses came (*va'yavo moshe*), and told the people all of God's words and all the laws," *va'yavo* seems to mean, as it did in 19:7, "brought back," the implication being, in both instances, that he descends from the mountain. But, as noted also, as regards 19:7, that implication produces uneasiness. And as regards 24:3, it seems to produce at least uncertainty, because it may be that Moses has not been on the mountain at all because he descended in 19:25, just before the spoken Revelation began; and that in 24:3 he simply "came" out of the mist he has been in since 20:18, at the base of the mountain, learning the laws that, in fulfillment of God's first command, he teaches the Jews in 24:3.

That task done, in 24:9, in fulfillment of the second command, issued in 24:1, he "went up" (*va'yaal*) the mountain, in the company of Jewish leaders. But then he is again instructed to ascend, and the text repeats three times that he obeys. In 24:12, though he seems to be on the mountain, God says again, "Come up to Me, to the mountain." In response, in 24:13, "Moses went up on God's mountain." In 24:15, he "reached the mountain top." (There is no warrant for this translation by Kaplan, because the Hebrew says simply, "He went up the mountain.") And in 24:18, he "climbed to the mountain top." (Once again, the Hebrew says simply, "He went up the mountain." And because in Kaplan's translation Moses reaches the top of the mountain in 24:15, even in his rendering 24:18 seems to repeat 24:15.)

The uneasiness and uncertainty that inhere in the problem of where Moses is located when the second of God's commands is issued and fulfilled are, as noted, not even the most significant part of the puzzlement that inheres in the response of Moses to the second command. Because concerns in the verbal pattern relating to ascent and descent established during the episode of the spoken Revelation reappear when the second command is issued and fulfilled, it is not possible to know whether or not Moses is on Mount Sinai when the second command is issued; or why he is repeatedly said to be on the mountain when the second command is fulfilled. That is problematic. But the response of Moses to the second command is more deeply problematic, because, as noted, he delays fulfilling the command in order to perform an action that he seems to devise; because many of the details of his action are problematic; and because, when the delay ends, many details of how he fulfills the command are problematic.

The action Moses seems to devise occurs in 24:3-8, immediately after God commands him to ascend the mountain, first in the company of others, then alone. Only after he completes the action does he fulfill God's command, when he ascends, in 24:8-11, in the company of others, and, in 24:12-18, alone. And both the action and its aftermath are problematic.

The command to ascend the mountain received, Moses should, it seems, ascend at once, as instructed in 24:1, "along with Aaron, Nadav and Avihu, and seventy of the elders of Israel." Instead, in 24:3-8, he proceeds as follows:

> [3] Moses came and told the people all of God's words and all the laws. The people responded with a single voice, "We will keep every word that God has spoken." [4] Moses wrote down all of God's words. He got up early in the morning, and built an altar at the foot of the mountain, along with twelve pillars for the twelve tribes of Israel. [5] He sent the [consecrated] young men among the Israelites, and they offered oxen as burnt offerings and peace offerings to God. [6] Moses took half the blood [of the offerings], and put it into large bowls. The other half he sprinkled on the altar. [7] He took the book of the covenant and read it aloud to the people. They replied, "We will do and obey all that God has declared." [8] Moses then took [the rest of] the blood and sprinkled it on the people. He said, "This is the blood of the covenant that God is making with you regarding all these words."

Why Moses performs the action above, in precisely the way he does, seemingly at his own initiative, the Torah does not say. Nor does it establish conclusively when the action occurs. And a number of its details are problematic.

The first of the problematic details appears in 24:3, when Moses relates to the people two clearly distinguished categories of utterances: "all of God's words (*et kal divrei hashem*) and all the laws (*v'et kal hamishpatim*)." What is contained in each of these categories is not clear; nor is it clear why the Jews commit "to keep" only the first; especially because Moses seems to relate to them almost nothing except "the laws," the *mishpatim*, that God says, in 21:1, he "must set before [the Israelites]," and that He teaches Moses from 21:1 to 23:33, a moment before Moses speaks to the Jews. Nor is it clear which of His words are meant by "all of God's words."

Other details are also problematic. Why, in 24:4, Moses writes down "all of God's words" (*et kal divrei hashem*), but not "all the laws" (*v'et kal hamishpatim*), is not clear. Nor is it clear in what book he writes them, or why. It may be a book related to the covenant that God asserts, in 19:5-8, He is making between Himself and the Jewish people; though no book related to that covenant is mentioned until 24:7, when it is referred to as "the book of *the* covenant" (*sefer ha'brit*), though no antecedent exists for the definite article in "the book." Nor is it clear why, the next morning, the altar built and the sacrifices in progress, in 24:7 Moses repeats to the Jews what he told them the day before, this time by reading from "the book of the covenant," rather than by speaking to them; or why they repeat their commitment, once again, excluding the *mishpatim*, by specifying they will keep only "all that God has declared" (a misleading translation by Kaplan of the Hebrew, which seems to maintain the distinction between the two categories of utterances, and should read "all of God's words"). It is not clear from the Hebrew in 24:7 whether Moses reads from the book, or all of the book. It is not clear whether, given the exclusion of the *mishpatim* in the Jews' commitment, the book even contains a reference to the *mishpatim*. That it may not seems indicated by Moses' assertion, in 24:8, after he sprinkles blood on the Jews, that the covenant has been made "regarding all these words," rather than the *mishpatim*. Indeed, it is not clear what is written in the book. Nor is it clear whether the fact that Moses reads, rather than speaks, is significant; or why, when he addresses the Jews a second time, in 24:7, they add to their initial commitment, in 24:3, to "keep" all of God's words the commitment also to "obey" them. (Why Kaplan translates the same Hebrew word, *naaseh*, as "keep" in 24:3 and as "do" in 24:7 is not clear.)

His action completed, in 24:9 Moses goes up the mountain, accompanied, as instructed in 24:1, by "Aaron, Nadav and Avihu, and seventy of the elders of Israel." And in 24:10-11 they experience a vision that is almost entirely mysterious:

> [10] They saw a vision [*va'yiru*] of the God of Israel, and under His feet was something like a sapphire brick, like the essence of a clear [blue] sky. [11] [God] did not unleash His power against the leaders of the Israelites. They had a vision [*va'yeicheizu*] of the Divine, and they ate and drank.

Whether or not "they" include Moses is not clear. What exactly they see is not clear. Nor is it clear why God seems to consider unleashing His power against them, because He grants them the vision, and they seem to do nothing wrong; unless they should not be eating and drinking after experiencing a vision. But if that is the case, "though" and "nonetheless" should be inserted in 24:11, and its two sentences should, it seems, be recast as follows:

> [God] did not unleash His power against the leaders of the Israelites, though they had a vision [*va'yeicheizu*] of the Divine, and nonetheless ate and drank.

Finally, what difference, if any, exists between *va'yiru* and *va'yeicheizu* is not clear.

The vision experienced, in 24:12-18, to fulfill God's command, Moses continues, alone, up the mountain:

> [12] God said to Moses, "Come up to Me, to the mountain, and remain there. I will give you the stone tablets, the Torah and the commandment that I have written for [the people's] instruction." [13] Moses and his aide Joshua set out. Moses went up on God's mountain. He said to the elders, "Wait for us here until we return to you. Aaron and Chur will remain with you. Whoever has a problem can go to them." [15] As soon as Moses reached the mountain top, the cloud covered the mountain. [16] God's glory rested on Mount Sinai, and it was covered by the cloud for six days. On the seventh day, He called to Moses from the midst of the cloud. [17] To the Israelites, the appearance of God's glory on the mountain top was like a devouring flame. [18] Moses went into the cloud, and climbed to the mountain top. Moses was to remain on the mountain for forty days and forty nights.

The definite article in "the stone tablets" is problematic, because it presumes an antecedent, but none exists. The difference between "the Torah and the commandment" is not clear. Nor is it clear why God speaks of a single commandment, or which commandment it is. The use of "the stone tablets" in series with "the Torah and the commandment" is problematic, because the tablets are where God has written the Torah and the commandment. And if that is so, the preposition "on" (*ba*) and a shift in word order would seem necessary, so the sentence would read, "I will give you the Torah and the commandment that I have written on the stone tablets for [the people's] instruction." The sudden appearance of Joshua, in 24:13, and then of Chur, in 24:14, is problematic, because they are not mentioned, in 24:1, among the company who ascend with Moses. It is not clear where Joshua "set out" from, where he goes, or why. Moses' instruction to the elders, in 24:14, should, it seems, precede his ascent in 24:13. It is not clear from the Hebrew whether "the cloud" in 24:16 covers the mountain, or Moses. Nor is it clear that Moses, or anyone else, knows how long he will be on the mountain. God tells him, in 24:12, that he will "remain" there; but does not say for how long. Moses tells the elders, in 24:14, to wait until he and Joshua "return to you." But he does not say when he will return. In 24:18 "forty days and forty nights" are specified; but neither to Moses nor to the Jews.

On the question of where Moses is located when the spoken Revelation occurs opinion is divided. Abarbanel asserts that he is standing with the Jews at the base of Mount Sinai, and explains that God wants him there to caution the Jews yet again not to cross His boundary. Alshich agrees, and offers four explanations of why God wants Moses to be at the base of the mountain. In his commentary on 19:24, Sforno also agrees that Moses is standing with the Jews, as does Ramban in his commentary on 24:3. Neither Sforno nor Ramban says why God wants Moses with the Jews. On the other hand, in his commentary on 19:25 Ibn Ezra asserts that, after Moses finishes warning the Jews not to cross God's boundary, he and Aaron go up the mountain, and then the spoken Revelation begins.

On the question of whether in 20:18 Moses ascends the mountain, or simply enters into the mist—that is to say, on the question of *nigash*—opinion is also divided. In his commentary on 19:24, Sforno asserts that Moses remains with the Jews at the base of the mountain continuously from 19:25 to 24:9, when he fulfills the first part of God's second command in 19:24 by ascending the mountain in the company of Aaron. In his commentary on 24:3, Ramban seems to agree. Alshich agrees with Sforno, and notes that the mist into which Moses enters is located at the base of Mount Sinai. In his commentary on "Moses came" in 24:3, Ibn Ezra asserts that, at some point after 23:33, Moses comes down from the mountain he ascends at 19:25. (Ibn Ezra does not explain how the people can speak to Moses in 20:16, if he is on the mountain, nor does he comment, in 20:18, on *nigash*.) In his commentary on "Moses came" in 24:3, Malbim asserts that *nigash* means Moses ascends the mountain at 20:18, and comes down in 24:3 to teach the Jews the laws God has taught him from 20:19 to 23:33. (That being the case, Malbim must agree with Abarbanel, Sforno, and Ramban that during the spoken Revelation Moses is at the base of the mountain with the Jews; because Moses cannot ascend both at 19:25 and at 20:18.) In his commentary on "Moses came" in 24:3, Ralbag asserts that Moses comes down from the mountain. He does not seem to say when Moses ascended it.

On the question of why, after Moses completes his action, and ascends the mountain in the company of leaders of the Jews, he is again commanded to ascend, opinion is also divided; as it is on the related question of why the fact that he does ascend is stated three times.

In the opinion of Rashi, which follows from his commentary on 24:1, the ascent in 24:9 occurs on a different day than does the descent on 24:14; so the instruction to ascend in 24:12 is distinct from the instruction to ascend in 24:1. In his commentary on 24:12, Ramban agrees that two days are involved, and thus two separate ascents, but disagrees about which days they are (because Ramban contends that the events narrated in 19:1 to 24:18 occur in chronological order). Daat Mikrah, Sforno, Abarbanel, and Ibn Ezra assert that the instructions to ascend in 24:1 and in 24:12, and the ascents in 24:9 and 24:13, are elements of a single event. Daat Mikrah asserts that in 24:9 Moses ascends Mount Sinai with a number of Jewish leaders, descends with them after they have experienced their mysterious Revelation, is commanded in 24:12 to ascend again, and in 24:13 does so. In his commentary on 24:12, Sforno asserts that "come up" (*alei*) in 24:12 commands Moses to continue ascending, to the top of the mountain (and thus is presumably different from the same word, *alei*, in 24:1, which means simply, "come up"). Abarbanel agrees with Sforno, as does Ibn Ezra in his commentary on 24:12.

None of the opinions above explains why the text asserts twice again—in 24:15 and 24:18—that Moses "went up" (*va'yaal*). In his commentary on 24:18, Chizkuni asserts that *va'yaal* means "to the top of the mountain". (He does not discuss the earlier uses of the word.) And his assertion is undermined by the fact that when the text intends "the top of the mountain" it says so explicitly, as is underscored by the juxtaposition of "on the mountain top" in 24:17 and *va'yaal el hahar* in 24:18, which means literally, "[Moses] went up the mountain."

Of the action that Moses performs after God teaches him the two laws about proper worship and the wide range of civil laws detailed in 20:19-23:33, only the first part seems obviously required by God. About details of even that part opinions differ. That God does not require the rest of the action—that He may not have commanded it—seems not to have been noticed. And opinions differ about details of the rest of the action, and of its aftermath.

Because he is commanded in 20:19 and 21:1 to teach the Jews the laws God teaches him in 20:19-23:33, Moses must tell them, in 24:3, "all of God's words (*et kal divrei hashem*) and all the laws (*v'et kal hamishpatim*)." But, as differences of opinion underscore, it is not clear what the words in the two categories of utterances mean, or what the differences between the categories are. Nor is it clear what the response of the Jews means.

In the opinion of Rashi, the first category, "all of God's words," refers not to the two laws about public worship detailed in 20:19-23, but to two instructions related to preparing for the Revelation at Mount Sinai; and the second category, "all the laws," refers to the Noachide Laws, the seven laws binding upon gentiles. According to Sforno, the first category refers to everything that God says from 19:3 to 20:23, from the moment, the Jews having encamped at Mount Sinai, God begins commanding Moses what to say to them to the moment He finishes teaching Moses the two laws about public worship; and the second category refers to the laws (*hamishpatim*) first mentioned in 21:1 that God teaches Moses from 21:1 to 23:33. Malbim, Abarbanel, Daat Mikrah, and Ralbag agree with Sforno. According to Ibn Ezra, the first category seems to refer to all of the positive and negative commandments contained in the book of the covenant mentioned in 24:7, and the second category seems to refer to the laws detailed in 21:1-23:33. Ramban does not distinguish between the two categories; he simply asserts that Moses teaches the Jews everything God taught him from 20:19 to 23:33. Saadia Gaon includes in the first category everything that God commanded the Jews, without specifying what that means; and he does not mention the second category.

In his commentary on 24:4, Ralbag asserts that Moses records the response of the Jews to his teaching in a book, without specifying which book. Daat Mikrah concurs, and adds that traditionalists have offered many opinions (*dayot rabot v'shanot*) regarding the matter. Ibn Ezra asserts that the reference is to the book of the covenant first mentioned in 24:7. If that is the case, it is not clear why it is not identified as the book of the covenant in 24:4, or why it is rendered in 24:7 with the definite pronoun, because the book is mentioned for the first time in 24:7, and thus, as noted, no antecedent exists. Nor is it clear why a book is necessary for the sealing of a covenant; especially because no book is involved in the covenants discussed and sealed in Genesis.

Some of the differences of opinion among traditionalists regarding the details of the sacrifices that are brought are discussed by Nachshoni.[5]

Some of the differences of opinion regarding what the book of the covenant contains are summarized in the following footnote by Kaplan to 24:7:

> Some say that this includes all of Genesis and Exodus up to the giving of the Ten Commandments (Rashi; *Mekilta* on 19:10). According to others, it was all the laws discussed up until this point (*Mekilta loc. cit*), particularly 21:1-23:19 (Ramban; Ibn Ezra on 23:4; Hirsch), or the admonitions in Leviticus 25:1-26:46 (*Mekilta*; Chizzkuni). Others say that it was the Ten Commandments (Rabbi Yehudah HaChasid, quoted in *Paneach Raza*) or the verse, Exodus 19:5 (*Midrash Hagadol*; Bachya).

5. Yehuda Nachshoni, *Studies in the Weekly Parshah* (New York, 1994-2001), vol. 2, pp.518-520.

As the summary shows, none of the traditionalists cited considers the possibility that the book contains either, or both, of the categories of utterances discussed above. In the commentary on 24:7, Daat Mikrah asserts that it contains the second of the category of utterances. In the opinion of Sforno, the addition of "obey" (*v'nishmah*) in 24:7 to the Jews' commitment in 24:3 to "keep" (*naaseh*) God's commandments bespeaks their intention to keep the commandments because they want to obey God. In the opinion of Daat Mikrah, they commit to "keep" when Moses reviews from memory God's laws, and commit to "obey" when he reads from the book of the covenant. Rashbam asserts that "keep" refers to laws already given, whereas "obey" refers to laws that will be given. Chizkuni concurs, as does Abarbanel; who adds that "obey" may refer to the commitment of the Jews to obey an angel who will guide them through the desert. Malbim also concurs; and adds that "keep" may refer to immediate obedience to God's laws, and "obey" to subsequent efforts to understand them. Ralbag asserts that "keep" refers to laws that require action (that the Jews "do" something), whereas "obey" refers to laws (primarily negative laws) that do not require action. Ibn Ezra offers three different commentaries on the differences between "keep" and "obey," one of them a gloss on the opinion of Saadia Gaon, who asserts that the Jews respond first with "obey," then with "keep."

As noted, when Moses performs the action detailed above is not clear. In his commentary on 24:1, Rashi asserts that the action occurs before the Revelation at Mount Sinai, in response to God's command, in 19:11, that Moses "sanctify" the Jews. In Rashi's opinion, based on Mechilta on 19:10, the sanctification is effected by the sacrifices and by Moses' resort to the book of the covenant. The necessity of moving 24:1-11 to 19:14, where Moses "sanctified" the Jews, is not problematic for Rashi, because he invokes without reservation, as other traditionalists do, the dictum that *ein meuchar umukdam batorah*—that the Pentateuch does not always proceed in chronological order.

In his commentary on 24:1, Ramban, who invokes the dictum as infrequently as possible, asserts that Moses' action occurs after the Revelation; that, indeed, all of the events from 19:1 to 24:18 occur in chronological order.

As Nachshoni shows in detail,[6] the disagreement between Rashi and Ramban is a microcosm of the disagreement between two schools of traditionalists; and, he concludes (517), it "cannot be decided in favor of either, since the text can be read both ways."

---

6. Ibid., vol.2, pp. 514-517.

Most traditionalists concerned with the matter assume that God's command to Moses, in 24:1, to go up Mount Sinai accompanied by "Aaron, Nadav and Avihu, and seventy of the elders of Israel" fulfills His command to Moses, in 19:24, to go up "along with Aaron." (Why that should be assumed is not clear, because in 19:24 only Aaron is mentioned.)

Some of the differences of opinion about the nature of the vision Moses' companions experience on the mountain, about why they afterwards eat and drink, and about why God may consider unleashing His power against them, are summarized by Nachshoni.[7]

Daat Mikrah notes that no antecedent seems to exist for "the stone tablets" in 24:12, and speculates (*v'efshar*) that the definite article betokens compression of language, or the possibility that the text has omitted some previous mention of the tablets.

On the related questions of what is written on the stone tablets, and what the differences are between "the Torah and the commandment," opinion is divided. Daat Mikrah suggests two possibilities: that the stone tablets contain "the Torah and the commandment . . . written for [the people's] instruction" still in the mind of the Author but unspecified; or that they contain only the Ten Pronouncements. Rashi asserts that the tablets contain only the Ten Pronouncements, but that hints of all six hundred and thirteen of the laws God mandated are contained in them. In the opinion of Sforno, "the Torah" refers to the theoretical portion (*hacheilek ha'iyuni*) of the Pentateuch, and "the commandment" to its practical portion (*hacheilek hamaasi*). Ibn Ezra asserts that both "the Torah" and "the commandment" refer to the Ten Pronouncements; "the Torah" to the first and the fifth of them, and "the commandment" to the other eight. Rashbam agrees. In the opinion of Malbim, the phrase "the stone tablets and the Torah" refers to the Pentateuch, and "the commandment" refers to the Mishnah. Rabbenu Bachya concurs. In the opinion of Abarbanel, "the stone tablets" refers to the Written Torah, and "the Torah and the commandment" refers to the Mishnah. Alshich asserts that "the Torah" refers to the Mishnah, and "the commandment" refers to the *divrei sofrim*, the laws derived from the thirteen hermeneutical rules revealed, according to traditionalists, at Mount Sinai.

In an opinion in Berachot 5a, each of the relevant phrases in 24:12 refers to a specific text, as follows:

---

7. Ibid., vol. 2, pp. 520-521.

R. Levi b. Chama says further in the name of R. Simon b. Lachish: What is the meaning of the verse: *And I will give thee the tables of stone, and the commandment, which I have written that thou mayest teach them?* 'Tables of stone': these are the ten commandments; 'the law': this is the Pentateuch; 'the commandment': this is the Mishnah; 'which I have written': these are the Prophets and the Hagiographa; 'that thou mayest teach them': this is the Gemara.

(That "the commandment" is in the singular and must therefore refer to only one commandment is not noted by the traditionalists above.)

In the opinion of Daat Mikrah, Joshua is not in the company that ascends the mountain with Moses in 24:9, and therefore does not experience the mysterious Vision in 24:10-11. He is with Moses in 24:13, because it would be undignified for Moses to begin unescorted his ascent to the top of the mountain. Rabbenu Bachya agrees that Moses' dignity requires an escort. (Neither Daat Mikrah nor Rabbenu Bachya explains why the escort should be Joshua.) In the opinion of Ramban, Joshua is in the company that ascends the mountain in 24:9, and does experience the mysterious Vision. Ralbag agrees; as does Alshich, who adds, as does Ramban, that only Joshua escorts Moses in 24:13, because he is superior spiritually to the rest of the company. Rashi says he does not know why Joshua is with Moses, because he cannot accompany him to the top of the mountain.

According to Daat Mikrah, it seems (*mistaber*) that Chur is not in the company that ascends with Moses in 24:9. Ibn Ezra thinks it possible (*ulei*) that he is among the company in 24:9. Alshich asserts that Chur is superior spiritually to the elders mentioned in 24:14. Rashi, referencing Sotah 11b, asserts that Chur is Moses' nephew, the son of his sister, Miriam. Abarbanel says that Chur is an expert judge.

Except perhaps for Abarbanel, none of the traditionalists above says why Chur suddenly appears, or why he is considered spiritually superior to the elders. And why Abarbanel says Chur is an expert judge is not clear.

In its commentary on 24:14, Daat Mikrah notes that Moses' instruction to the elders in 24:14 must precede his ascent in 24:13. But why the verses do not appear in reverse order is not discussed.

Daat Mikrah also notes that, in 24:14, Moses does not specify to the elders when he "will return." That being the case, it is not clear why virtually all traditionalists assert that Moses and the Jews know that he is to be on Mount Sinai for forty days; especially because that information is provided neither to Moses nor to the Jews.

Reason and Mystery in the Pentateuch

To understand the ascent of Moses onto Mount Sinai to receive a document written by God, it is necessary to understand where Moses is during a number of moments before, during, and after the spoken Revelation occurs, where the mist is located into which Moses enters after the spoken Revelation occurs, to be taught a series of laws by God, whether the mist is the same as the thick cloud, why, after Moses has learned the laws, and taught them, from memory, to the Jews, he does not fulfill at once God's command that he ascend Mount Sinai, why, instead, he writes in a book seemingly related to a covenant, then performs an action involving a series of sacrifices and related actions many of whose details are unclear, whether the action occurs before, or after, the Revelation occurs, what he tells the Jews when he teaches them the laws God has taught him, whether they are divided into two categories of utterances, if they are, what laws are contained in each of the categories, why, when they respond to Moses, the Jews seem to ignore the second of the categories, into what book Moses writes, what he writes in the book, why the sacrifices must be brought precisely as described, why the Jews respond differently when Moses teaches the laws from memory and when he reads them from the book, what he reads from the book, why he repeats what he teaches by reading from the book, what the nature is of the vision experienced by the leaders who accompany Moses, after he performs his action, part way up the mountain, why God seems to consider unleashing His power against the leaders, what, if anything, they have done wrong, what is contained in the document God has written and will give to Moses when he ascends the mountain by himself, why Joshua appears when Moses begins the ascent, why Moses chooses Chur to serve, while he is on the mountain, as one of judges of difficult cases, why, when the ascent seems completed, the text repeats twice that Moses ascends, whether Moses knows—or whether the Jews know—how long he is to remain by himself on the mountain.

If these matters cannot be understood, it is not possible to establish the plain meaning of the narrative that describes them. But they cannot be understood.

⁌

The apparently straightforward narrative of the rebellion of Korach and his cohort masks concerns that often, perhaps even typically, make it impossible to understand what motivates the rebels, and how the rebellion unfolds.

The verses in which the rebellion begins, Numbers 16:1-3, are problematic for a variety of reasons:

> [1] Korach son of Yitz'har (a grandson of Kehoth and great-grandson of Levi) began a rebellion along with Dathan and Aviram (sons of Eliav) and On the son of Peleth, descendants of Reuben. [2] They had a confrontation with Moses along with 250 Israelites who were men of rank in the community, representatives at the assembly, and famous. [3] They demonstrated against Moses and Aaron, and declared to them, "You have gone too far! All the people in the community are holy, and God is with them. Why are you setting yourselves above God's congregation?"

It is not clear why the lineage of the various rebels is presented. Nor, as a more literal translation than Kaplan's of 16:1-2 indicates, is it clear how the rebellion coalesces:

> [1] Korach son of Yitz'har (a grandson of Kehoth and great-grandson of Levi) took (*va'yikach*), and Dathan and Aviram (sons of Eliav) and On the son of Peleth, descendants of Reuben, [2] and they rose up (*va'yikahalu*) against Moses, and 250 Israelites who were men of rank in the community, representatives at the assembly, and famous.

Apparently, Korach, Dathan, Aviram, and 250 distinguished Jews join forces against Moses. But it is not clear what *va'yikach* means, why it is in the singular, whereas *va'yikahahlu* is in the plural, or why the 250 distinguished Jews appear after both verbs. That is to say, it is not clear why the verses do not assert that Korach, Dathan, Aviram, and 250 distinguished Jews took (*va'yikchu*), in the plural, and rose up (*va'yikahahlu*).

It is not clear to whom the rebels are referring in 16:3 when they assert that "all the people in the community (*ha'eidah*) are holy, and God is with them."

It is not clear why, in 16:4, before responding to the rebels, Moses "threw himself on his face."

It is not clear whether, in the first of his responses to the rebels, the test proposed by Moses to the cohort who demand the priesthood represents his own will, or the will of God, because, the demand advanced, Moses responds not by relating, in his usual manner, what God commands, but what, it seems, he himself wishes to be done, as regards not only the substance of the test, but its specific details.

The first of his responses to the rebels is divided into two sections. In the first section, 16:5-7, he outlines a test of the validity of their apparent complaint; and in the second, 16:8-11, he explains, in effect, why they should not take the test. Both sections are problematic in several regards.

The seemingly unambiguous assertion in 16:5 that Moses addresses all of the rebels turns out, when the test is detailed in 16:6-7, to be incorrect. There seem to be too many words in 16:5. And the test seems a non sequitur, because it seems entirely unrelated to the rebels' complaint:

> [5] Then he spoke to Korach and his whole party. "[Tomorrow] morning," he said, "God [will show that He] knows who is His and who is holy, and he will bring them close (*va'yakriv*) to Him. He shall choose those who shall [be allowed to] present [offerings] (*yakriv*) to Him. [6] This is what you must do: Let Korach and his entire party take fire pans. [7] Tomorrow place fire on them, and offer incense on them before God. The man whom God chooses shall then be the holy one. You sons of Levi have [also] gone too far!"

In 16:5 Moses seems to address Korach, Nadav, Avihu, On, and the 250 distinguished Jews. But that is not the case because, as 16:7 indicates, Moses is addressing only the Levites among the rebels, the "sons of Levi," that is, the descendants of Levi; and so, he cannot be addressing Nadav, Avihu, and On, who are descendants of Reuben, or any of the 250 distinguished Jews who are not Levites. (At least one of the 250 must, it seems, be a Levite, because Moses is addressing sons of Levi, in the plural, and among the rebels other than the 250 only one, Korach, is a Levite.) That being the case, it is not clear how many rebels Moses is addressing in 16:5-7. Nor is it clear whether in 16:8, translated literally—"Moses said to Korach, 'Listen to me, please, you descendants of Levi'"—Moses is addressing only Korach, or the rebellious Levites.

Moses' prediction, in 16:5, about what God will do in the morning seems repetitious, because the second of its assertions seems to repeat the first one; though that is clear only from a translation more literal than Kaplan's, which would read: "And the person whom He chooses He will bring close to Him." That Moses uses the same verb—as can be seen above, a form of *l'hakriv*, to bring close—in both assertions, underscores that 16:5 seems to say twice that God will bring close to Himself the person He chooses. (Because Kaplan's translation in 16:7—that God will choose a man, rather than a number of men—supports the more literal translation in 16:5—that God will choose a single person—it is misleading to speak, as Kaplan does in 16:5, of a number of men—of "them"—whom God will choose, or of "those" who will serve Him. And there is no warrant in the Hebrew for Kaplan's translation of the closing sentence of 16:5.)

As a response to the complaint of the rebels in 15:3 that Moses has usurped political authority, his proposal, in 16:5-7, that they determine through the test who, in God's opinion, so to speak, should rule the Jews seems to make no sense, because the sacrifice Moses describes seems entirely unrelated to the question of authority; because, in fact, any sacrifice would seem entirely unrelated to that question. Therefore it cannot be that Moses is responding to the complaint, "We want to share political authority with you" by saying, "Offer a sacrifice, and we will see if you may." But that response does make sense if Moses understands that the rebels' complaint is not that he refuses to share political authority with them, but that he refuses to let them serve as priests. And Moses does understand that, as the test he proposes implies, and as he asserts explicitly in the second section of his response. But why Moses understands it—why he disregards the rebels' rhetorical question in 16:3, and responds to the complaint it masks—is not clear.

The response of Moses to Korach and the other rebellious Levites seemingly complete, three abrupt shifts in scene occur, all of them problematic. In 16:12-14, Moses suddenly shifts his attention from Korach to Dathan and Aviram; then, in 16:15-17, he seems to shift back to Korach and the other rebellious Levites; and, in 16:18-19, it is morning, and the test of Korach and the other rebellious Levites begins.

The sudden shift to Dathan and Aviram (but not also to On, who has disappeared, without explanation) underscores the concern in the assertion in 16:5 that Moses addresses his initial response "to Korach and his whole party." As noted, in 16:5-11 he seems to address his response only to Levites; that is to say, only to Korach and to the unspecified number of Levites among the 250 distinguished Jews. And that seems corroborated by the assertion in 16:12 that Moses "sent word to summon Dathan and Aviram, the sons of Eliav," who apparently were not present when he addressed Korach and the 250 distinguished Jews.

The sudden shift in 16:12-14 also assigns to Dathan and Aviram a justification for rebellion different from that assigned them in 16:3. As noted, the complaint made by Korach and the other Levites that Moses has usurped authority masks a demand to serve as priests; the same complaint made by Dathan and Aviram should, it seems, be taken at face value. Unlike Korach and his cohort of Levites, they do seem to object to the political authority exercised by Moses. But why they object is not clear, because they justify themselves in two ways. In 16:3 the justification is theological: that because "all the people in the community are holy, and God is with them," Moses and Aaron cannot justify "setting yourselves above God's congregation." But, in 16:13-14, it is entirely mundane, as the outburst directed at Moses shows:

> [13] "Isn't it enough that you brought us out of [Egypt], a land flowing with milk and honey—just to kill us in the desert! What right do you have to set yourself above us? [14] You didn't bring us to a land flowing with milk and honey, or give us an inheritance of fields and vineyards. Do you think you can pull something over our eyes? We will definitely not come!" (*lo naaleh*)

Because the theological argument reflects the interest of Korach and his cohort of Levites in degrees of proximity to God, it is tempting to suppose that only they advance that argument. But, as the verbs in 16:3 and Moses' response in 16:5 indicate, all of the rebels, including Dathan and Aviram, seem to advance it. And thus it is not clear how Dathan and Aviram do justify their rebellion.

Nor is it clear why they begin their outburst as they end it, by asserting *lo naaleh*, which translated literally means, "We will not ascend!"

Because in 16:15 Moses seems to be responding angrily to the outburst of Dathan and Aviram, it is not immediately clear that in his attention seems to have shifted abruptly once again, back to Korach and his cohort of Levites.

> [15] Moses became very angry. He prayed to God, "Do not accept their offering. I did not take a single donkey from them! I did not do any of them any harm!"

Though it seems reasonable to suppose that Moses becomes "very angry" at Dathan and Aviram, because they have just refused his summons (or, literally, his order that they "ascend," whatever that means), in fact, as the opening of his prayer indicates, he must, it seems, be angry at Korach and his cohort of Levites, because only they, it seems, are planning to offer sacrifices. Thus, it cannot be immediately clear that he has, it seems, abruptly stopped speaking to Dathan and Aviram.

His closing remarks of the day to Korach and his cohort of Levites in 16:16-17, which detail instructions regarding the sacrifices to be brought, seem repetitious, because they seem more or less the same as the instructions detailed in 16:6-7. Even the explicit information in 16:17 that Aaron also will offer a sacrifice seems implied in the assertion in 16:7 regarding "the man whom God chooses."

It is not clear from the description, in 16:18-24, of the events on the morning of the test that precede the destruction of the rebellion whether the rebellion has corrupted anyone other than the 254 rebels, because it is not clear how, if at all, as those events unfold, the meaning of the noun *ha'eidah*, the community, shifts. The apparent repetition in 16:19 of the assertion in 16:18 that Korach and his cohort gather at the entrance to the Communion Tent may indicate that other Jews also gather there.

> [18] Each one took his fire pan, placed fire on it, and then offered incense. They stood at the Communion Tent entrance along with Moses and Aaron. [19] Then, when Korach had rallied his whole party (*kal ha'eidah*) to the Communion Tent entrance, God's glory suddenly became visible to the entire community (*el kal ha'eidah*).

Because there is no warrant in the Hebrew for Kaplan's translation, which renders *ha'eidah* first as Korach's "whole party," and then as "the entire community," *kal ha'eidah* in 16:19 may indicate that the entire community of Jews joins at The Communion Tent with Korach's cohort, already there at 16:18, and that God's glory appears to all of them.

That indication seems to be supported by the effort of Moses and Aaron, in 16:20-22, to dissuade God from annihilating everyone involved in the rebellion, including Jews never before associated with it.

> [20] God spoke to Moses and Aaron saying, [21] "Separate yourselves from this community (*ha'eidah*), and I will destroy them in an instant." [22] [Moses and Aaron] fell on their faces. They prayed, "Omnipotent God of all living souls, If one man sins, shall You direct divine wrath at the entire community (*kal ha'eidah*)?"

Because almost beyond question Moses and Aaron are not praying that only Korach ("one man") and not his cohort be punished, they must, almost beyond question, be imploring God not to punish the entire community (*kal ha'eidah*), either because they are innocent, or because they have been corrupted by Korach. And that is how their prayer is understood, in 16:23-24, because

> [23] God spoke to Moses, telling him to [24] announce to the entire community (*el ha'eidah*), "Withdraw from the pavilion of Korach, Dathan, and Aviram."

But how and when Korach corrupted them—if he did—is not clear. And so what—if anything—they are guilty of is not clear.

During the two climactic actions of the rebellion—in 16:31-34, all of the rebels are buried alive except the 250 distinguished Jews, and in 16:35 they are burnt to death—it is not clear what, if anything, happens to Korach.

Finally, it is not clear why, in 17:1-3, God commands that instruments of a mortal sin against Himself be incorporated into the Tabernacle. The rebellion crushed,

> [1] God spoke to Moses, saying, [2] "Tell Eleazar (son of Aaron the priest) that the fire pans have been sanctified, and he must gather them up from the burned area. He shall then scatter the burning coals far and wide. [3] The fire pans belonging to the men who committed a mortal sin have been presented before God and thus sanctified, so he shall make them into beaten plates to cover the altar. Let this be a sign for the Israelites."

That God wishes the fire pans preserved as a warning to the Jews not to rebel is understandable. But why the fire pans have been sanctified through participation in sin is not clear. And therefore it is not clear why they should become an integral part of divine service by becoming covers for the altar in The Tabernacle.

Rashi, Ramban, and Ibn Ezra agree (as do virtually all of the traditionalists concerned with the matter) that the lineage of the rebels is presented to explain why the rebellion occurs. But Ibn Ezra's explanation differs from that of Rashi and Ramban. (Virtually all of the other traditionalists side with Ibn Ezra or with Rashi and Ramban.)

According to Ibn Ezra, Korach is honored when, by God's command in Numbers 3:44-51, Levites replace first-born Jews of every tribe, and he and the members of his tribe are separated out from the rest of the community, to minister to the priests in the Tabernacle when the priests offer sacrifices. But he regards this honor as insufficient, because he resents that the priesthood itself is assigned, in his opinion by Moses, rather than by God, to Aaron and his sons. And Dathan and Aviram resent that the first-born are replaced by the Levites, because they are descendants of Reuben, the first-born son of Jacob, and therefore, after 3:44-51, conclude they have been demoted spiritually; because before 3:44-51, they were, according to Ibn Ezra, the priests who offered sacrifices.

According to Rashi and Ramban, referencing Midrash Tanchumah, Korach resents a perceived slight by Moses related to his lineage. According to Ramban, Korach is also jealous of Aaron. And Dathan and Aviram come to resent the loss of their birthright.

Kehoth, Korach's grandfather, sired Amram, Itzhar, Hebron, and Uzziel (listed, in order of birth, in Exodus 6:18). Korach knows that the status of Moses and Aaron, the sons of Amram, the eldest son of Kehoth, is legitimate. But he resents deeply that, in 3:30, Moses appoints Eltzafan prince of the Kohathites, though, as Exodus 3:22 confirms, Eltzafan is the middle son of Uzziel, the youngest of the sons of Kehoth, whereas he, Korach, is the eldest son of Itzhar, Kehoth's second-born.

Why Korach is jealous of Aaron, Ramban does not say.

In Ramban's opinion, Dathan and Aviram do not initially resent the loss of the birthright, because they understand that, as Genesis 48:5 confirms, Jacob transferred it from Reuben to Joseph. They join the rebellion because, as they complain in 16:12-14, they will end up corpses in the desert, not prosperous masters of Canaan. But a series of reverses that occur in the desert after 3:44-51 rouses their annoyance at the demotion they experience at 3:44-51; so they join forces with other first-borns, similarly annoyed.

(In the opinion of Ibn Ezra, who does not believe that the Pentateuch always proceeds in chronological order, the rebellion occurs after the first-born are replaced by the Levites, in 3:44-51; whereas, in the opinion of Ramban, who favors chronological order, it occurs after the disastrous spying expedition detailed in 13:1-14:45.)

The question of how the rebellion coalesces turns on the use of the verb *va'yikach*, Korach "took." According to Rashi the verb is not transitive in 16:1, and therefore does not require a direct object; it is reflexive, and indicates that Korach disassociates himself physically from the community. According to Ramban, it indicates that Korach becomes the slave of his rebellious heart. According to Rabbenu Bachya, he becomes adamantly attached to his grievances. According to Alshich, Korach takes—that is to say, claims—the position he feels entitled to as the son of Itzhar. According to Or Hachayim, Korach takes stock of his chances of succeeding in a rebellion against Moses. According to Malbim, he takes stock of the reasons that justify his rebellion. According to Sforno and Rashbam, *va'yikach* is transitive, and indicates that Korach, Dathan, Aviram, and On take 250 men, as the first step in fomenting the rebellion. According to Ibn Ezra, it is only Korach who takes the 250 men. According to Chizkuni, Korach takes Dathan, Aviram, and On. According to Abarbanel, Korach, Dathan, Aviram, and On take—in effect, seduce with their arguments into rebellion—the members of the tribe of Reuben, and, from members of the other tribes, 250 distinguished Jews.

According to Rashi, the assertion by the rebels in 16:3 that "all the people in the community are holy" refers to the community of Israel, all of whom, the rebels argue, heard the Revelation at Mount Sinai. Ibn Ezra and Or Hachayim agree; and add that, in further asserting that "God is with them," the rebels argue further that God's glory has been with them all since it first enveloped them all at Mount Sinai. According to Abarbanel, Rabbenu Bachya, and Chizkuni, when the rebels assert that "all the people in the community are holy" they are referring to the first-borns, who, as noted, were separated out from the rest of the community in Exodus 13:2. But Abarbanel also considers the possibility that "all the people" may refer to the entire community. According to Kli Yakar, "community," *eidah*, refers to every group of ten Jews. Every such group is considered to be holy, and to be enveloped by God's glory; and Moses has, in the opinion of the rebels, without justification subjugated all of the Jews by systematically usurping authority over each *eidah*.

According to Rashi, Moses falls on his face in 16:4 because he is unsure whether he can appeal to God yet again to overlook yet another rebellion, and therefore is distraught. According to Alshich and Or Hachayim, he falls on his face to show that he is humble, and has never wanted the position of authority God has assigned him. According to Ibn Ezra, he falls into a prophetic trance. According to Ramban, he prays to be told how to proceed. Rashbam agrees; and adds that God does tell him how to proceed. According to Chizkuni, he covers his face because he is embarrassed (at what, Chizkuni does not say), prays, and is told by God what to say to Korach. According to Kli Yakar, referencing Sanhedrin 110a, Moses falls on his face because he hears the rebels are hinting that he is prone to adultery.

According to Ibn Ezra, the test proposed by Moses to the cohort of Korach demanding the priesthood may represent the will of God, if in 16:4 Moses falls on his face into a prophetic trance, in which he learns about the test; or it may be that Moses falls on his face of his own volition (for reasons Ibn Ezra does not specify). In the opinion of Abarbanel, it may be that Moses devises the test by himself; or God may command him to propose it. According to Chizkuni and Rashbam, in 16:4 Moses falls on his face to pray for guidance, and God responds with the test He has devised. According to Malbim, commenting on 16:18, Korach mistakenly supposes that Moses has devised the test on his own. According to Ramban, commenting on 16:5, Moses does devise the test on his own; though not precisely on his own, because he is prompted by *ruach hakodesh*, a degree of divine guidance.

In the opinion of Rabbenu Chananel, all of the 250 distinguished Jews are Levites; so only what happens to Nadav, Avihu, and On while Moses is addressing all of the other rebels is not clear. Ramban, in his commentary on 16:5, criticizes Rabbenu Chananel sharply, and asserts that the rebels are recruited from all twelve of the tribes. Chizkuni and Abarbanel agree. According to Rashi and Rabbenu Bachya, most of the 250 are recruited from the tribe of Reuben. According to Alshich, the only Levite among the rebels is Korach, and thus none of the 250 is a Levite. Thus (unless the opinion of Rabbenu Chananel is accepted) it is not clear how many rebels Moses is addressing.

According to Rashi, in 16:8 Moses first addresses only Korach, in a conciliatory fashion, but then, finding him adamant, addresses the other Levites, hoping to persuade them not to rebel with him. According to Ibn Ezra and Chizkuni, in 16:8 Moses addresses only the Levites, rather than, as in 16:5-7, all of Korach's cohort. According to Ramban, in 16:8 Moses addresses only Korach, but mentions the other Levites, hoping they will desist from rebellion. According to Alshich, in 16:8 Moses talks to the Levites about the rebelliousness of Korach. According to Rabbenu Bachya and Malbim, the first part of 16:8 refers to Moses' address, in 16:5-7, to Korach and his entire cohort regarding the diminished spiritual status of the first-borns, whereas the second part refers to the complaint of the Levites regarding the priesthood.

According to Ramban, the appearance of repetition in 16:5 indicates that God makes two separate assertions: that in the morning Aaron will be separated out from the others trying to offer sacrifices; and that his descendants alone will be similarly separated out, forever. According to Or Hachayim, God may be responding to two separate arguments advanced by Korach: that others are better qualified than Aaron to serve as High Priest; and that because others are as qualified, they also should be designated as High Priests. According to Sforno, God first asserts that Aaron alone will be designated High Priest, and then warns that anyone who contests the designation will be punished.

According to Ramban, Moses' assertions in 16:5 show that in his wisdom (*b'chachmato*) he grasps that Korach is challenging the designation of Aaron as High Priest, rather than demanding that Moses share political authority with him. But how Moses grasps Korach's motive—how his wisdom produces the insight that Korach's words mask what he wants—Ramban does not say.

The first of the three abrupt shifts in scene mentioned above, in 16:12-14, is problematic because it is not clear why Moses must summon Dathan and Aviram, because, as noted, in 16:5 he begins addressing "Korach and his whole party," a cohort that, it seems, includes Dathan and Aviram. According to Daat Mikrah, it seems likely (*mistaber*) that while Moses addresses Korach, some (*achadim*) of the other rebels, Dathan and Aviram presumably among them, depart; and that therefore in 16:12 Moses orders that they be summoned. (According to Malbim, in his commentary on 16:12, as Moses addresses "Korach and his whole party," Dathan and Aviram depart because they realize Moses is responding only to the complaint regarding the shift of the priesthood from the descendants of Reuben to those of Levi; and as that matter does not interest them, because they do not aspire to priesthood, they depart.) According to Rashi and Ramban, Moses seeks out Dathan and Aviram a second time, to persuade them to desist. According to Or Hachayim, Moses speaks only to Dathan and Aviram, in the hope that flattering them with a private audience will persuade them to desist. According to Alshich, after Moses silences Korach, he sends for Dathan and Aviram, to persuade them that the rebellion is unjustified. According to Abarbanel, after Moses explains to Korach that his claim to the priesthood is unjustified, he calls Dathan and Aviram, to justify the loss of the birthright of their ancestor Reuben, Jacob's oldest son.

According to Rashi, the words *lo naaleh* ("We will not ascend!") that open and close the response of Dathan and Aviram to Moses indicate that they are about to stumble: to suffer a downfall, rather than an ascent. According to Ibn Ezra, Moses is asking them to meet him at the Tabernacle, which is located in a high place, and to which they must therefore literally ascend; or he is calling upon them to serve God, a call to spiritual ascent. According to Rabbenu Bachya, the first of Ibn Ezra's explanations is correct. According to Chizkuni and Rashbam, *naaleh* indicates a summons to court. According to Abarbanel, by *lo naaleh* Dathan and Aviram express their conviction that they will never ascend to Canaan, but will die in the desert. In the opinion of Or Hachayim, the words indicate that they refuse a private audience with Moses, because they think that he is unfit to exercise political authority. According to Kli Yakar, the words indicate that they refuse to meet with him because they suspect he intends to bribe them to desist.

About whether the second of the abrupt shifts mentioned above, in 16:15-17, occurs traditionalists disagree, as their disagreement about the object of Moses' anger shows. According to Alshich and Or Hachayim, in 16:15 Moses becomes "very angry" not at Korach and the rest of the rebels, but at Dathan and Aviram. Ibn Ezra agrees. Ramban agrees that Moses becomes very angry at Dathan and Aviram, but does not think that they are planning to offer sacrifices in the morning. According to Rashi, Moses becomes very angry at Korach and his cohort for planning to offer sacrifices. Rabbenu Bachya seems to assert that Moses becomes very angry at all of the rebels. According to Abarbanel and Malbim, he becomes very angry at Dathan and Aviram. Daat Mikrah seems to agree that Moses becomes very angry at Dathan and Aviram; but is puzzled that he pleads with God not to accept their sacrifices in the morning, because they are not among the cohort planning to offer sacrifices.

According to Or Hachayim, in 16:16-17 Moses repeats the instructions to the rebels that he detailed in 16:6-7 because they do not, in the interval between the two sets of verses, accept his rebuke and desist. According to Malbim, the two sets of instructions differ in two respects: Aaron does not appear in the first set, and Dathan and Aviram are excluded from the second. According to Ibn Ezra, in response to 16:16-17 the rebels take their fire pans, and the test Moses detailed in 16:6-7 begins. According to Ramban, verses 16:16-17 are necessary because the rebels are reluctant to proceed to the test without the explicit assurance, absent from verses 16:6-7, that Aaron will participate in it. Moreover, according to Ramban, the instructions in 16:6-7 include Dathan and Aviram, whereas the instructions in 16:16-17 exclude them; because in the interval between the two sets of verses Dathan and Aviram infuriate Moses so deeply, he wishes them to suffer a far more ignominious death than will befall the other rebels.

According to Malbim, in 16:18 the 250 distinguished Jews who presume to offer sacrifices gather (*va'yamdu*) at The Communion Tent, whereas in 16:19 Korach rallies (*va'yakheil*) the entire Jewish community there, inciting it against Moses. According to Rashi, Korach spends the night before the test inciting each of the tribes in turn. Alshich, Abarbanel, Baal Haturim, and Rabbenu Bachya agree that Korach rallies the entire Jewish community against Moses. According to Or Hachayim, in 16:18 the 250 distinguished Jews merely gather in front of the Communion Tent, but they—and not the entire Jewish community—do not denounce Moses until Korach incites them, in 16:19, to do so. According to Kli Yakar, commenting on 16:21, Korach does not convince the entire Jewish community to denounce Moses. According to Ralbag, only the 250 distinguished Jews denounce Moses.

According to Kli Yakar, Rabbenu Bachya. and Rabbenu Chananel, Moses misunderstands the reference in 16:21 to "this community" (*ha'eidah*), thinking it signifies that God intends to destroy the entire Jewish community; so God explains that He intends to destroy only the rebels. Sforno agrees that He intends to destroy only the rebels. According to Abarbanel and Ramban, God intends to destroy the entire Jewish community; all of them deserve to die, because, seduced by Korach, they denounce Moses. According to Malbim, in so doing they deny, in effect, that God has sent Moses, and that he is a true prophet; therefore they deserve to be destroyed. According to Daat Mikrah, at the minimum Moses and Aaron are convinced that God intends to destroy the entire Jewish community. According to Alshich, all of them are deeply impressed by Korach's slander of Moses, and therefore deserve to be destroyed, but are spared because Moses disabuses them before God destroys the rebels.

According to Rashi, commenting on 17:2, the fire pans "have been sanctified" because they were used by the rebels to offer sacrifices, and therefore can serve only a sacred purpose such as to cover the Tabernacle. According to Ramban and Daat Mikrah, also commenting on 17:2, and Ralbag and Ibn Ezra, commenting on 17:3, the fire pans have been sanctified, but because, as 17:3 asserts, they were presented "before God," and not because they were instruments in the illicit action of rebels. According to Sforno, commenting on 17:3, and Daat Mikrah and Malbim, commenting on 17:2, the fire pans were sanctified for legitimate purposes, and therefore can be used to cover the Tabernacle, though the rebels misused them. Or Hachayim, commenting on 17:3, seems to agree with Sforno and Daat Mikrah. According to Alshich, commenting on 17:2, the fire pans have been sanctified by participation in the test that ends with the destruction of the rebels at the Tabernacle. According to Abarbanel, the fire pans have not been sanctified. They have undergone a process that would have ended in sanctification had the motives of the rebels not been evil; or they were set aside, so that the process of sanctification could begin.

To understand the rebellion of Korach and his cohort, it is necessary to understand, from the brief statement about their lineage, precisely what their complaints against Moses are, precisely how and why Korach convinces them to rebel, to which tribes they belong, how Moses knows that a complaint apparently about political authority masks a demand for the priesthood, how many of the rebels Moses addresses in his first response to their complaint, where the other rebels go while that response is unfolding, why, after the response ends, Moses falls on his face, whether a test he proposes for the following morning at the Communion Tent is his own idea, or God's, why he seems to say twice that God's response to the test will show whom He favors, why Dathan and Aviram seem to be rebelling for two unrelated reasons, why they begin and end their statement of the second of their reasons by insisting that they will not come to Moses, why God seems to think (if He does) that all of the Jews are part of the rebellion and therefore deserve to be destroyed, why the fire pans used by the rebels at The Communion Tent are turned, by God's command, into sacred objects. But it is not possible to understand these matters.

⸺

The opening verses of Deuteronomy, 1:1-5, announce a task. But for three chapters, until 4:1, the task is deferred, while a complicated memory is recounted. The recourse to memory is problematic per se, as are important details of the memory. And why the task is deferred is not clear.

The task, that Moses teach a number of God's commandments to the Jews, is announced as follows:

> [1] These are the words that Moses spoke to all Israel on the east bank of the Jordan, in the desert, [and] in the Aravah, near Suf, in the vicinity of Paran, Tofel, Lavan, Chatzeroth and Di Zahav. [2] [This is in the area] which is an eleven-day journey from Horeb to Kadesh Barnea by way of the Seir highlands. [3] On the first of the eleventh month in the fortieth year, Moses [also] spoke to the Israelites regarding all that God had commanded him for them. [4] This was after he had defeated Sichon king of the Amorites who lived in Cheshbon, and Og, king of Bashan, who lived in Ashtaroth, [who was defeated in] Edre'i. [5] Moses began to explain this law on the east bank of the Jordan, in the land of Moab, saying:

As the colon at the end of 1:5 underscores, Moses is about to begin teaching law. But he does not begin until 4:1. Instead, he recounts a memory.

That he does so is problematic. To traditionalists it is axiomatic that, as God's scribe, Moses simply records all of the Torah (except possibly, in an opinion recorded in Bava Basra 15a, the closing lines of Deuteronomy, which describe the death of Moses). But that means that in Deuteronomy, from 1:6 to 4:1—from the assertion that "Moses began to explain this law, saying" to the moment Moses says, "Now Israel, listen to the rules and the laws that I am teaching you to do"—Moses records not what his memory, acting autonomously, evokes while he stands at the east bank of the Jordan, but what God causes his memory to evoke. That being the case, it does not seem possible to ask why Moses remembers what he does, in the order he does, and thus what the act of memory says about him. But because it does not seem possible either to ask why God evokes in Moses the memory He does, it is impossible to know how to understand the act of memory.

(The possibility that God did not dictate Deuteronomy to Moses, but that Moses himself wrote it, and God approved of it, is discussed below.)

The memory itself is problematic, for three reasons. First, it is not clear what relation, if any, exists between the events Moses recounts. Second, it is not clear why he focuses with especial intensity on a spying mission, why he conflates the disastrous consequences of that mission and an event that occurred thirty-eight years afterwards, or why he seems to recall incorrectly important details of the spying mission (and of a judicial innovation). And third, it is not clear why Moses berates his audience for having responded sinfully to the mission, because no one in his audience did respond to it.

The recounting, which occurs, as 1:3 states, during the fortieth year after the Exodus, concerns both events that occurred thirty-eight years earlier, when the Jews left Mount Sinai, and recent events. Moses begins by recounting God's command, thirty-eight years earlier, that the Jews invade Canaan at once, and His assurance that they will conquer it with ease. He then recounts the judicial innovation, and the spying mission, the Jews condemned by their response to it to thirty-eight years of wandering and death in the desert, often among antagonistic tribes. That done, he moves forward thirty-eight years, and recounts the opening successes in the invasion, which has at last begun.

It would be interesting to know—but it is not possible to know—why, of the seminal history he lived through, Moses remembers only the events above, in the order he does—or why God causes his memories to unfold as they do—or why God dictates, and Moses records in Deuteronomy, only those memories, in that order. As God's servant, Moses inflicts the plagues on Pharaoh, leads the Exodus, parts the Sea of Reeds, witnesses the drowning in it of the Egyptian army, provides water for the Jews in the desert, occasions the fall of the manna from heaven, experiences the Revelation at Mount Sinai, spends forty days, at least twice, and perhaps three times, alone with God on the top of the mountain, endures the transgression of the Golden Calf, oversees the construction of the Tabernacle, and speaks with God, face-to-face, within it. And yet, of all those events (and others), Moses remembers, at the beginning of Deuteronomy, only the events mentioned above, in the order above. (He remembers the Revelation in 5:1-19.) And why that is so cannot be known, because neither Moses nor God explains the matter.

Nor is it possible, for the same reason, to know why his attention is riveted by the spying mission, a primary focus of the act of memory; or why he seems to confuse it with another event, and seems to remember imprecisely important details of it (and of the judicial innovation).

The seeming confusion is striking. During the second year after the Exodus, as preparation for the invasion of Canaan, in Numbers, 13:1-14:38 Moses sends twelve spies to reconnoiter the country. Because the Jews believe a pessimistic report brought back by ten of the spies, and therefore berate God and refuse to invade Canaan, God condemns to death in the desert all of the adult males among them (except the two spies who speak optimistically); and by the fortieth year after the Exodus, all of them are dead. During that fortieth year, in Numbers, 20:7-13, Moses offends God by striking with his staff a rock that will provide the Jews water if, as God commands, he speaks to it. As punishment, God condemns him also to death in the desert; and several months later, he is dead. As can be seen, the two events—the spying mission, and Moses' transgression at the rock—are completely distinct, and separated by thirty-eight years. Yet when Moses recounts the spying mission, in Deuteronomy 1:34-40, he seems to conflate to it his transgression at the rock.

> [34] When God heard what you said, He angrily swore, [35] "No man of this evil generation will see the good land that I swore to give your fathers. [36] The only exception will be Caleb son of Yefuneh. Since he followed God wholeheartedly, not only will he see it, but I will give him and his descendants the land he walked." [37] God also displayed anger at me because of you [and] He said, "You too will not enter [the land]. [38] Joshua son of Nun, who stands before you, will be the one to enter, and he will give Israel their hereditary property. [39] The ones to enter the [land] will be the children whom you feared would be taken captive and your little ones who even now do not know good from bad. To them I will give [the land] and they will occupy it. [40] You must now turn around and head into the desert toward the Southern Sea."

In the passage above, Moses seems unmistakably to imply—indeed, in effect seems to say—that God condemned him to die in the desert during the second year after the Exodus, when He condemned the adult male Jews to the same fate during the spying episode. But, as Moses must know, that was not the case; he was condemned thirty-eight years later, a few months before he speaks in the passage above, for the entirely unrelated transgression of striking a rock with his staff. Why, therefore, Moses seems to associate God's anger at himself and His anger at the Jews is not clear.

Neither is it clear why Moses seems to remember incorrectly important details of the spying episode. In the recounting, Moses asserts, in 1:22, that the Jews suggested that the spies be sent; in 1:23 that he approved of the suggestion; and in 1:25, that the spies presented an optimistic report. And, as noted, in 1:37-38 he seems to imply that God was angry at him for some unspecified transgression related to the spying. But these assertions are at odds with assertions in the narrative of the relevant events in Numbers. There, in 13:1-2, God suggests that the spies be sent. There is no evidence that Moses approves (or disapproves) of the suggestion. The report begins optimistically in 13:25-27, but turns pessimistic in 13:26-33. And—perhaps most striking—there seems to be no evidence that God becomes angry at Moses, or punishes him for any transgression related to the spying.

Nor is it clear why Moses seems to remember inaccurately important details of the judicial innovation that eases a difficult burden of leadership. In 1:9-17 in the narrative in Deuteronomy, because it has become increasingly difficult for him to resolve increasingly frequent disputes between Jews, Moses suggests, and the people agree, that a system of lower and higher courts be devised, staffed by judges they will designate and he will appoint, an arrangement that will free him to adjudicate only the most difficult of disputes. But these assertions seem at odds with the history narrated in Exodus. There, in 18:1-26, the innovation is suggested by Jethro, Moses' father-in-law, when he visits Moses in the desert, notices that he holds court all day, asserts that if he continues to do so he will exhaust himself and the Jews, and suggests to Moses, who agrees, that the system of courts described above be devised (the judges, though, not to be designated by the people).

It is not clear why, during the recounting, Moses berates his audience for a litany of transgressions no one listening to him committed, mainly in the disastrous response, in 1:26-45, to the report of the ten pessimistic spies. Everything he says about the response is true. But everyone guilty of it—every Jew (except Joshua and Caleb) who was an adult male when the spies returned—is dead, killed by God during thirty-eight years of retributive wandering in the desert. As Moses himself says, in 2:14-16, the recounting occurs when

> [14] the generation of warriors had died out from the camp, as God had sworn. [15] God's hand had been directed specifically against them so that they would be finished. [16] It was at this time that all of the men of war among the people finished dying.

That being the case, it is not clear why Moses continually uses the second-person in addressing his audience, as, for example, when he complains in 1:26 that, after hearing the spies' report, "You did not want to head north [to Canaan] . . . and you rebelled against God your Lord." Their elders refused to head north, and in consequence died. But no one in his audience refused to head north. Nor did any of them rebel against God. In fact, they did nothing wrong during the first two years after the Exodus. And because of the subsequent thirty-eight years almost nothing is known, (a matter to be discussed) it is not possible to understand why Moses berates them.

Finally, it is not clear why the recounting occurs. Commanded by God to begin expounding law to the Jews, Moses should, it seems, have proceeded at once from 1:5 to 4:1, "Now, Israel, listen to the rules and laws that I am teaching you to do." Instead, he evokes, for himself and his audience, an event thirty-eight years in the past that still absorbs him, framed by a number of seemingly unrelated events. And it is not possible to understand why he does that, because he does not say; or why God, who also does not say, instructs him to record the memory in His book.

About why Moses focuses intently on the spying episode, about the mix of events that frame it, about why the recounting occurs, and about the fact that he berates an audience that did not sin during the spying episode, or perhaps even in the thirty-eight years afterwards, traditionalists do not seem to speak.

About the recourse to memory per se they speak obliquely, when they discuss the difference between Deuteronomy and the four other books of the Pentateuch. Perhaps the most intriguing elements of that discussion (reviewed by Nachshoni)[8] are the assertion by Or Hachayim that whereas Moses served as God's scribe vis-à-vis the other four books, he wrote Deuteronomy by himself, not at God's command; and the assertion by Kli Chemdah that Moses shaped Deuteronomy by himself, and that God read the Book and approved it.

---

8. Ibid., vol. 5, pp. 1188-1190.

In his commentary on Deuteronomy 1:1 to the words "Moses began" in 1:5, Ramban seems to agree with Or Hachayim.

At the outset of his commentary on 1:37—"God also displayed anger at me because of you"—Kli Yakar acknowledges that most traditionalists have been unable to explain why Moses in effect asserts, while recounting the spying episode, that God then condemned him to die in the desert together with the ten miscreant spies and the generation of adults they misled. And indeed the assertion cannot, it seems, be explained.

Perhaps therefore, a number of prominent traditionalists reiterate the assertion. Thus, Sforno, Malbim, Or Hachayim and Kli Yakar, citing various verses in Numbers, 11:14-34, assert that, by the second year after the Exodus, Moses is aware that he will not enter Canaan.

But none of these traditionalists asserts that God condemns Moses during the spying episode because He is angry with him. And thus they do not explain 1:37. All of them present variations of a single argument: that the Jews are severely diminished spiritually by their disastrous response during the spying episode; that they might have been rehabilitated spiritually at the episode of the rock, had Moses' faith not wavered during that episode; and that therefore God becomes angry at Moses. But that means that God becomes angry at Moses during the fortieth year in the desert, and that does not explain why Moses in effect asserts, in 1:37, that God became angry at him thirty-eight year earlier, during the second year after the Exodus.

Or Hachayim admits as much, acknowledging that his long and complicated commentary on 1:37, based on *biglalchem* ("because of you"), is homiletic, and does not seem to explain the plain meaning of the text, because there is no evidence that God was angry at Moses during the spying episode.

Malbim admits much less. He is astonished (*tamu m'od*) at the reference to the episode of the rock in 1:37, because it occurred thirty-eight years after the spying episode. But he does not acknowledge that his subsequent assertion—that God's condemnation of Moses during the spying episode is conditional, and becomes irrevocable only when his faith wavers during the episode of the rock—does not explain why, in Moses' apparent opinion, God became angry with him during the spying episode.

Kli Yakar does not acknowledge that his explanation is subject to the same objection. And Sforno simply asserts that God condemns Moses during the spying episode, without discussing when He becomes angry with him.

In the opinion of Ramban, in 1:37 Moses berates the Jews for persisting in sin through the thirty-eight years that separate the two episodes. But because almost nothing is known of the thirty-eight years after the spying episode, it is difficult to understand why Ramban asserts the Jews sinned during those years, and therefore deserve to be berated. Moreover, as Or Hachayim notes, because 1:37 is embedded in a long recounting of the spying episode, it is difficult to believe that the recounting is interrupted for one sentence so thirty-eight years of transgression can be reviewed.

In the opinion of Ibn Ezra, in Numbers 13:2 God does not command that spies be sent to Canaan. He merely consents to the suggestion of the Jews, in Deuteronomy, 1:22, that they be sent. Thus, in his opinion, the seeming conflict between Numbers 13:2 and Deuteronomy 1:22 reflects a process, not a contradiction.

Expanding on Ibn Ezra's opinion, Rashi asserts that, in Deuteronomy 1:22, the Jews make the suggestion. In 1:23, Moses appears to approve. Therefore, in Numbers 13:2, God consents. Thus, Moses and God consent to a suggestion that is inappropriate, because it shows that the Jews do not have faith enough in God, who has promised (for example, in Deuteronomy 36:21-22) that they will easily conquer Canaan. Moses' assertion, in 1:23, "I approved," should therefore not be taken at face value. It means, to begin with, that Moses approves, but that God does not. But not even Moses approves; he only seems to, says Rashi, following Sifri, in the hope that his seeming consent will prompt the Jews to withdraw the suggestion.

In his commentary on Numbers 13:2, Ramban agrees that Moses disapproves of the Jews' suggestion, but only insofar as it bespeaks insufficient faith; insofar as it bespeaks a wish to prepare for specific battles by reconnoitering (a wish that reflects a praiseworthy desire not to rely on miracles), Moses does approve of the suggestion. Moreover, Ramban denies that Moses asks God to approve the spying mission, or that God does approve it. In Ramban's opinion, Moses does not consult God about the spying mission per se. Ramban rejects Rashi's opinion that God issues no command related to the mission. He denies implicitly that God consents to Moses' approval of the Jews' suggestion. But he asserts that God commands Moses to send not, as is customary in such matters, a total of two spies, but one spy from each tribe.

Rashi's opinion that God issues no command derives from His interpretation of *le'cha* ("for yourself") in Numbers 13:2, "send out men for yourself." Malbim disagrees, asserting, in the questions he poses at the outset of his commentary on Numbers 13, that God does issue commands regarding the mission.

Or Hachayim agrees with Rashi, who references the opinion of Sotah 34 that *le'cha* indicates consent rather than command.

In the opinion of Sforno, *le'cha* indicates that God cautions Moses not to allow the Jews to choose the spies, but to choose them himself, and thus to assure they will be distinguished men.

Kli Yakar accepts the opinion of Sforno regarding *le'cha*, but offers six other possible meanings of the word.

In the opinion of Kli Yakar, God's assertion to Moses—"Send out men (*anashim*) for yourself (*le'cha*)"—indicates that Moses can, if he cares to (*le'cha*), send men, but that they will turn out to hate Canaan. God would have sent women (*nashim*), who love His land.

In the opinion of Rashi and of Malbim, who references Sifri, only two of the spies, Joshua and Caleb, assert, in Deuteronomy 1:25, "The land that God our Lord is giving us is good." But that does not explain why Moses refrains from recounting the pessimistic report of the other ten spies.

In the opinion of Or Hachayim, Moses does not refrain. He does not refer to the report explicitly, because he is anxious not to rouse God's wrath against his audience. But he does allude to it, through verbal echo, repeating in Deuteronomy 1:25 the words that appear in Numbers 13:26, "The report that they brought back was . . . ."

In the opinion of Ramban, the ten spies discuss their findings first in a public meeting with the Jews and Moses, and then in secret meetings with the Jews; and Moses recounts only the public meeting, in which they present only the good news that Canaan is a bountiful land. Because no evidence of secret meetings exists in Numbers 13, Ramban in effect argues that the recounting there must be modified in the light of evidence he adduces from Deuteronomy 1:27, "You protested in your tents."

Siftei Chachomim agrees that the ten spies present only good news in 1:27, but does not explain when, in the recounting, they present pessimistic news.

Sforno asserts that even the ten spies admit that Canaan is bountiful. But he does not explain why the recounting omits their pessimistic news.

The seeming inaccuracies in Moses' recounting of the judicial innovations instituted in the desert are discussed by Ramban and Malbim.

In his commentary on Deuteronomy 1:18, Ramban offers three explanations of why Moses, who knows that the innovation was Jethro's idea, asserts that it was his own. For a complicated reason, his humility prevents him from crediting his father-in-law. Or he does not wish to publicize the fact that he is married to a Cushite woman. Or, for reasons not specified, God commands him not to credit Jethro.

In his commentary on 1:6-21, Malbim notes that, in Exodus 18:1-26, Moses designates the judges, whereas in Deuteronomy 1:9-18, the Jews designate them; and that in Exodus 18:21 the candidates must be "God-fearing men—men of truth, who hate injustice," whereas in Deuteronomy 1:15 they must be "wise and well-known men from among your tribal leaders." In Malbim's opinion, the judges are designated both by Moses, who alone, aided by God, can penetrate the human heart and determine which candidates are "God-fearing," and by the Jews, who may know, through daily interaction, better than Moses which of their tribal leaders are "wise and well known."

(Various opinions different from Malbim's regarding the qualifications listed in Exodus 18:21 and Deuteronomy 1:15 are reviewed by Nachshoni.)[9]

In the opinion of Rashi, commenting on "and God will be with you" in Exodus 18:19, Moses asks God about Jethro's innovation, and institutes it only after God tells him that he should.

From the commentaries above, a composite can be fashioned. During his visit to Moses in the desert, Jethro suggests a judicial innovation. For a number of reasons, Moses claims the innovation is his own. And aided by the Jews, he institutes it; he himself checking for certain qualities in candidates for office, the Jews checking for others.

The composite is coherent. But whether, given the two texts, it is compelling, is not clear. Whether it really explains why Moses' memory of the innovation differs from the history of how the innovation was instituted is not clear. Whether, indeed, the difference can be explained is not clear.

To understand why the task announced at the outset of Deuteronomy is deferred so that a complicated act of memory can be recounted, it is necessary to understand why, set a task by God, Moses defers it, to remember, whether the sequence of the memories he recounts is governed by himself or by God, whether, indeed, God or Moses wrote the sections of Deuteronomy in which Moses recounts his memories, what, if anything, the process of remembering reveals about Moses, why one of the events—the spying episode—continues to absorb him thirty-eight years after it happened, why he attributes to it a dire consequence to himself that results from a

---

9. Ibid., vol.2, pp.464-469.

transgression he commits only months before he begins the recounting, why his memory of what the spies did and said, and how the Jews responded, and his memory of a crucial judicial decision, seem at odds with what seems to have happened, why he berates the Jews who hear the recounting for transgressions they did not commit.

It is not possible to understand the opening chapters of Deuteronomy without understanding the matters above. But it is not possible to understand them.

⸺

The discussions above, chosen at random, underscore the same fact: that in a significant number of instances, perhaps even typically, the plain meaning of the sacred history narrated in the Pentateuch cannot be established.

All of the discussions are incomplete. Many of the concerns all of them contain have not been noted. And only five short historical events, or short sections of them, have been discussed. A comprehensive survey of all of the similar concerns in all of the sacred history narrated in the Pentateuch would require an enormous work.

Such a work would corroborate the fact central to the present study: that in a significant number of instances, perhaps even typically, the language in which the sacred history in the Pentateuch is narrated precludes understanding of its plain meaning.

That fact must, in the opinion of the present study, be the indispensable beginning of traditionalist understanding, not only of sacred history, but also of the other major component of the Pentateuch, its codex. That is to say, the fact indispensable to discussion of sacred history in the Pentateuch is indispensable also to the study of law in the Pentateuch; therefore traditionalists must begin studying the codex by affirming that the language in which laws are mandated often, perhaps even typically, precludes understanding of what is mandated.

The necessity of that affirmation established, the present study discusses the response to the fact central to it that traditionalism necessitates, and why a counter-response derived from a view of reality antithetical to traditionalism should be considered with caution, especially as regards the futility of studying a specific set of laws, to be discussed.

⸺

Because understanding how, as both a theological and a practical matter, authority is vested in the codex depends upon understanding precisely what is meant by the Mishnah (the Oral Law), it is useful to begin with a contemporary statement regarding the Mishnah:

> The Torah [the Pentateuch] was accompanied by an authoritative tradition that explained the meaning of obscure passages and provided the rules and methods of accurately interpreting the text. Even a cursory reading of the Torah proves that such a tradition *had* to exist, for there is much more to the Torah than its written text.
> Examples:
>
> —the Torah prescribes that one who assaults his fellow must pay *ayin tachas ayin, an eye for an eye* (Exodus 21:24), yet never in Jewish history was physical punishment meted out for an assault. The verse was always understood to require monetary compensation. Surely Moses and his successors did not take it upon themselves to change the "plain" meaning of God's word.
>
> —Moses instructed the Jews to perform kosher slaughter *kaasher tziviticha, as I have commanded you* (Deuteronomy 12:21)—yet nowhere in the written text of the Torah do we find even one of the intricate and demanding rules of kosher slaughter. Where had He commanded them?
>
> Countless similar examples can be given. The implication of them is clear beyond a doubt: there is a companion to the Written Torah [*torah sheh b'al peh*] without which the Written Law can be twisted and manipulated beyond recognition, as indeed it has been by the ignorant through the centuries.[10]

This statement encapsulates a view unanimously endorsed by traditionalists, who, as noted at the outset of the present study, regard it as axiomatic that the Torah consists of the Written Torah, known as the Pentateuch, and the Oral Law, which accompanies it, known as the Mishnah, received, as the Pentateuch was, at Mount Sinai, transmitted orally without corruption for generations, and redacted as a text during the Babylonian exile by Rabbi Yehuda ha'Nasi, indistinguishable in theological authority from the Pentateuch, and thus not subject to debate when invoked as law mandated in the Pentateuch.

(The Mishnah, and the Gemara, that discusses it, constitute the Talmud.)

---

10 *The Chumash*, p. xxiii.

But the axiom, as regards the Oral Torah, must be precisely understood, because, as even a cursory glance at the Mishnah demonstrates, it cannot always—or even usually—mean what it means as regards the Pentateuch.

As noted, traditionalists must believe that the text of the Pentateuch they study is the text that God dictated to Moses at Mount Sinai. They need not believe that of the Mishnah; indeed, they cannot believe that of a good deal of it, as a brief glance at a particular Mishnah makes plain to common sense, and as Maimonides' classical statement regarding the structure of the Mishnah underscores as a theological matter.

It is, for example, not possible to assert that all three of the opinions below, recorded in the Mishnah in Berachot 2a, regarding the latest hour of the night at which an obligatory prayer known as the Shema ("Hear, O Israel") may be recited were dictated by God to Moses at Mount Sinai:

> From what time may one recite the shema in the evening? From the time that the priests enter [their houses] in order to eat their terumah until the end of the first watch. These are words of R. Eliezer. The sages say: until midnight. R. Gamliel says: until the dawn comes up. Once it happened that his sons came home [late] from a wedding feast and they said to him: We have not yet recited the [evening] shema. He said to them: If the dawn has not yet come up you are still bound to recite. And not in respect of this alone did they so decide, but whenever the sages say 'until midnight,' the precept may be performed until the dawn comes up . . . .. Why then did the sages say 'until midnight'? In order to keep a man far from transgression.[11]

Because the Mishnah records no dispute regarding the hour from which the evening Shema may be recited, common sense can accept that God told Moses at Mount Sinai that it may be recited from the time the priests entered the Temple to eat the portion of a certain sacrifice permitted to them. But common sense cannot accept that God told Moses at Mount Sinai the evening Shema may be recited until the end of the first of the three (in some opinions, four) watches into which the night is divided, and until midnight, and until dawn. Nor can it accept that God dictated to Moses on Mount Sinai the story the Mishnah tells about Rabban Gamliel and his sons, who lived some eighteen hundred years after the Revelation at Mount Sinai.

---

11. *The Babylonian Talmud* (London, 1990). Unless otherwise noted, all quotations are from this edition.

In the Introduction to Seder Zeraim, his overview of the Mishnah, Maimonides validates common sense. There are, he asserts, five categories of *mishnayot*.[12] In the first and second categories are laws that have never occasioned dispute. In that respect the laws in those categories are different in kind from the laws in the third, fourth, and fifth categories, which characteristically occasion dispute; and they differ from one another in that, though the laws in both categories were spoken by God to Moses, the Pentateuch contains hints regarding the laws in the first category, and those laws may be amenable to deductive reasoning, whereas the Pentateuch contains no hints regarding the laws in the second category, and those laws are not amenable to deductive reasoning. The laws in the second category are *halachah l'moshe mi'sinei*, "Laws Received by Moses at Mount Sinai." In the third category are "laws which are derived through deductive reasoning."[13] In the fourth category are *gezerot*, "decrees ordained by the prophets and Sages of every generation in order to make a protective fence around the Torah." And in the fifth category are *takanot*, "laws based on (empirical) investigation regarding the social behavior of individuals in those matters which do not constitute an addition to or detraction from a (Biblical) commandment—or regarding things which are efficacious for people with respect to the observance of the laws of the Torah."[14]

Only the laws in the first and second categories have absolute authority, because only those laws were spoken by God to Moses. As noted, the laws in the third, fourth, and fifth categories of the Mishnah also have absolute authority. But it derives from a different theological fact: that the Pentateuch itself—that is to say, that God Himself—assigned the authority to mandate law to a group of preeminent traditionalists, and to no one else. They alone were empowered, as regards the third category, by expertise in The Thirteen Principles of Exegesis, regarded axiomatically by Maimonides as *halachah l'moshe mi'sinei*, "Laws Received by Moses at Mount Sinai," as regards the fourth category by the commandment in Leviticus 18:30, "Keep My charge," and as regards the fifth category by the injunction in Deuteronomy 4:2, "Do not add to the word that I am commanding you, and do not subtract from it" and, as will be seen, by a statement in Deuteronomy 30:12. (They were empowered, in Exodus 23:2, to resolve disputes by majority

---

12. Moses Maimonides' Commentary on the Mishnah (New York, 1975), pp. 65-81.

13. *Ibid*, p.74.

14. Ibid, pp. 78-79. Words in parentheses are the translator's. They do not appear in the Hebrew text.

vote.) And their power was transferred, in perpetuity, exclusively to preeminent traditionalists in successive generations.

Because the source of absolute authority in the first and second of Maimonides' categories is different from its source in the third, fourth and fifth categories, the degree of truth in the first two categories is different from the degree of truth in the third, fourth, and fifth categories. Indeed, it is not accurate, as regards the latter, to speak of "truth," as opposed to "norm." Absolute truth is contained only in the laws in the first and second categories, because only those laws were told by God to Moses; and for traditionalists absolute truth is, by definition, the position that exists in the mind, so to speak, of God. In the third, fourth and fifth categories, by contrast, the preeminent traditionalists who mandate law in the Mishnah cannot have aspired to absolute truth, because, being merely human, they cannot have had access to the mind, so to speak, of God. And because that is the case, they must have been empowered to formulate only normative law, without regard to truth, as defined by traditionalism. Thus, for example, it is absolutely true that the commandment to extract "an eye for an eye" dictated by God to Moses at Mount Sinai never means literally an eye for an eye. And it is absolutely true that kosher slaughter must conform with commandments given by God to Moses at Mount Sinai—as noted, *kaasher tziviticha, as I have commanded you* (Deuteronomy 12:21)—as Moses, beyond question reiterating God's commands, commanded the Jews. By contrast, because God apparently did not tell Moses on Mount Sinai how late the evening Shema may be recited, and because absolute truth regarding that matter is in consequence inaccessible, the preeminent traditionalists empowered to mandate law in the Mishnah must have mandated only normative law concerning the matter, without regard to absolute truth.

Their task, as regards explicating the codex in the Pentateuch, is thus remarkably similar to the task of explicating the sacred history it records. Both task require that they distinguish between that which is absolutely true, and that which perforce provides only plausible speculation.

That Korach, for example, rebelled is absolutely true, because the Pentateuch—that is to say, God—asserted that he rebelled. But what precisely happened during the rebellion may often, perhaps even typically, be impossible to establish, because the written word of God often, perhaps even typically, precludes understanding. Traditionalists comment upon the details of the rebellion; but not to find absolute truth where the Author has rendered it impervious to understanding.

Similarly, that the Shema must be recited in the evening is absolutely true, because the Pentateuch—that is to say, God—commanded that it be recited. But about the details of the command that He has rendered impervious to understanding—for example, about until when it can be recited—only norms can be mandated.

In short, as regards both of the major components of the Pentateuch, sacred history and codex, traditionalists often, perhaps even typically, attempt to offer *an* explanation of an event in the Pentateuch, or *an* explanation of a legal mandate—a *plausible* explanation, not *the* explanation; not, that is to say, the truth that exists in the mind, so to speak, of God.

And, because that is the case, it is neither surprising nor inappropriate that, especially as regards the codex in the Pentateuch, the method of traditionalist inquiry is typically dispute; or that the effort to gain normative knowledge is more important than the effort, often, perhaps even typically, perforce foredoomed, to attain truth to a certainty.

Where truth is unattainable, the findings of any preeminent traditionalist—and of no one else—of any commentator who accepts the theological axioms associated with the Written Torah and the Oral Torah as defined at the outset of this study—of any commentator unreservedly devoted to the God who revealed the Torah, as the most precious of imaginable gifts, to the Jewish people—are valuable as efforts not (except when, as happens only very infrequently, He reveals some aspect of Himself) to understand Him, but to speculate plausibly about how, as regards the codex in the Pentateuch, His commandments must be fulfilled. Of the total effort of traditionalism as regards the codex it may, therefore, be legitimately said, as Eruvin 13b says of the disputes between the School of Hillel and the School of Shammai, *eilu va'eilu divrei elokim chayim*, "All of the findings represent the words of the living God"; not because any finding contains absolute truth, but because, except when, as is not often the case, God reveals His intention, traditionalists study the codex to understand the norms through which He may best be obeyed. And the study of that is, in the opinion of traditionalism, supremely impressive, without regard to what exists in the mind, so to speak, of God.

In the Gemara in Bava Metzia 59a-b, both the crucial importance of the study noted and its inherent limitation as regards absolute truth are underscored.

Rabbi Eliezer argues that a certain type of ceramic oven, known as a *tanur achnei*, is not susceptible to ritual impurity; the other preeminent traditionalists with whom he is disputing argue that it is susceptible to ritual impurity. The dispute proceeds as follows:

> On that day, Rabbi Eliezer used all the arguments in the world. But they [the sages] did not accept [them]. He said to them, "If the Halachah [the law] is in accordance with me, let this carob tree prove it." The carob uprooted and moved one hundred cubits from its place. They then said, "Proof cannot be brought from a carob tree." He then said, "If the Halachah is in accordance with me, let the channel of water prove it." The channel of water flowed backward. They said to him, "Proof cannot be brought from a channel of water." He then said, "If the Halachah is in accordance with me, let the walls of the house of study prove it." The walls of the house of study leaned, [and were about] to fall. Rabbi Kenosha rebuked [the walls], saying to them, "If Talmudic scholars argue with one another, what affair is it of yours?" [The walls] did not fall, out of respect for Rabbi Kenosha, nor did they straighten, out of respect for Rabbi Eliezer, and still remain leaning. [Rabbi Eliezer] then said, "If the Halachah is in accordance with me, let it be proved from Heaven." A heavenly voice went forth and said, "Why are you disputing with Rabbi Eliezer? The Halachah is in accordance with him in all circumstances." Rabbi Kenosha rose to his feet, saying, and "It [the Torah] is not in heaven." What [does it mean to say, quoting Deuteronomy 30:12, that] "the Torah is not in Heaven"? Rabbi Yirmeyah said, "[Since God] already gave the Torah on Mount Sinai, we do not pay attention to heavenly voices, for you [God] already wrote in the Torah at Mount Sinai (Exodus 23:2), 'After the majority to incline [resolve disputes regarding Halakhah by majority vote].'" [Generations later] Rabbi Natan met [the prophet] Elijah. He said to him, "What did the Holy One, blessed be He, do at that time?" He said, "[God] smiled and said, 'My sons have defeated Me, My sons have defeated Me!'"

As can be seen, only the preeminent traditionalists designated to do so, the sages, are authorized to determine what the law is. The quality of the arguments advanced against them does not matter; nor does the quality of their own arguments (if, as is not always the case, they advance arguments), or even the testimony of God. If they decide, by majority vote, that the *tanur achnei* is susceptible to ritual impurity, it is; and not even God may tell them otherwise, whether He testifies indirectly, by manipulating elements of nature, or directly, in His own voice. When they refuse to accept testimony from the carob, from the channel of water and from the walls, beyond question the sages understand that they are refusing to accept indirect testimony from God; and similarly as regards direct testimony, because beyond question they understand that the heavenly voice addressing them is the voice of God. Their spokesman, Rabbi Yehoshua, does not regard His testimony, in either form, as relevant to their effort to mandate binding law. Moreover, because Rabbi Eliezer asserts that the law should reflect his opinion seemingly because his arguments are decisive, and does not say he knows what is in the mind, so to speak, of God, and because God merely repeats Rabbi Eliezer's assertion, but does not say that Rabbi Eliezer knows what is in, so to speak, His mind, the dispute between Rabbi Eliezer and the sages is not a dispute about absolute truth, but about how normative law must be mandated, without regard to absolute truth. And God is unmistakably delighted with how the dispute unfolds and is resolved, because He is unmistakably delighted that the sages understand clearly the power He has vested in them, and are unafraid to assert it, even against Him.

Thus, as Maimonides asserts, the power to mandate binding law has been vested by God exclusively in a group of preeminent sages, whose authority is absolute. As regards the first two of Maimonides' categories, "Laws Received by Moses at Mount Sinai," *halachah l'moshe mi'sinei*, they transmit information handed down to them, verbally, and without corruption, from Mount Sinai. As regards the third, fourth, and fifth of his categories, they mandate law, because God has authorized them, and no one else, to mandate it.

The authority remains theirs exclusively to the present, and, as a theological matter, will never lapse. It is no longer, however, absolute authority—that is to say, authority derived directly from the Pentateuch, and thus from Revelation at Mount Sinai—because that order of authority apparently ended with the redaction of the Mishnah.

The termination of the absolute authority of the preeminent sages is indicated in *Mishneh Torah*, Maimonides' comprehensive codification of law, in Laws Concerning the Study of Torah, 1:11. A person, writes Maimonides,

> is obligated to divide his study time in three: one third should be devoted to the Written Law; one third to the Oral Law; and one third to understanding and conceptualizing the ultimate derivation of a concept from its roots, inferring one concept from another and comparing concepts, understanding [the Torah] based on

the principles of Biblical exegesis, until one appreciates the essence of those principles and how the prohibitions and the other decisions which were received from the oral tradition can be derived using them. The latter topic is called *Gemara*.[15]

By the Oral Law Maimonides unmistakably means only the Mishnah, as is clear from his Introduction to *Mishneh Torah*, which states that Judah the Prince transcribed into a book he called the Mishnah (*sefer ha'mishnah*) nothing but the Oral Law. the Gemara in Berachot 6a also asserts that the Mishnah and *torah sheh b'al peh* are synonymous terms, as does Shmuel Ha-Nagid in his Introduction to the Talmud that appears at the end of the tractate Berachot in the Vilna edition of the Talmud. And nowhere does the Talmud assert the Gemara—the commentary on the Mishnah, and by far the bulk of the Talmud—is part of the Oral Law.

Thus, as noted, the authority of the Mishnah is absolute and binding, whereas elaboration of it by preeminent traditionalists, typically through dispute, in the Gemara and afterwards, is only binding (except as regards *halahchah l'moshe mi'sinei*, "Laws Received by Moses at Mount Sinai"), and the formulation of law is an effort, not to locate absolute truth, but to establish, through commentary on the Pentateuch, legally binding norms of behavior. And thus it resembles the effort of traditionalists to establish the plain meaning of sacred history in the Pentateuch. Both efforts often, perhaps even typically, offer only plausible explanations; as has been shown above, of events primarily in the relation between God and His Chosen people; and as is shown in detail below, of the codex He has mandated, primarily to edify His Chosen People.

As regards, for example, the evening Shema, preeminent traditionalists consider not only the matter briefly discussed—how late it may be recited—but a number of other relevant matters. And whether they speak about these matters with absolute and binding authority, in the Mishnah, or with only binding authority, in the Gemara and afterwards, except in one matter they are not concerned with absolute truth; and so, except as regards that matter, it is possible to know what normative law is, but not whether normative law reflects absolute truth. That the evening Shema must be recited is absolutely true, because, as noted, in the Pentateuch God commanded that it be recited. But God did not speak plainly about how late it may be recited. Nor did He speak plainly about a number of details:

---

15. Moses Maimonides, *Mishneh Torah, Hilchot De'ot and Hilchot Talmud Torah* (New York: 1989), p. 172.

for example, in what position it may be recited, when, if ever, the recitation may be interrupted, whether reading constitutes recitation, whether recitation is valid if words are mispronounced, whether on his wedding night a bridegroom is exempt from reciting it. About these details, and others, God spoke only obliquely, or not at all. He may, indeed, not have said plainly even what excerpts from the Pentateuch comprise the Shema. That being the case, it is not possible, as regards at least the details mentioned, to know what He wants done; except that He wants relevant norms to be established, exclusively by preeminent traditionalists, and to be obeyed. And because, as noted, it is not possible to know which preeminent traditionalist, if any, has chanced upon the intention, so to speak, of God as regards at least any of the details mentioned, it is not possible to know whether obedience to the norms mandated constitutes, except indirectly, through obedience to the preeminent traditionalists, obedience to God.

Nor does it seem to matter. God, it seems, does not want the details of the recital of the Shema known to a certainty, any more than He wants it known to a certainty which of Joseph's brothers, if any, Joseph slanders, who the man (or the angel) is—or the angels are—he meets on his way to Dothan, who sells him into slavery in Egypt. What God seems to want is a range of plausible speculation presented by traditionalists regarding Joseph's history, and regarding the details of the Shema. In the first instance, no speculation need be preferred to any other; in the second, by contrast, a single authority empowered in perpetuity by God establishes normative behavior, commonly by choosing between two equally plausible options without regard to absolute truth as defined in the present study.

Precisely how that authority functions is evident from the discussion in the Gemara, of how late, in the Mishnah quoted above, the evening Shema may be recited.

The source in the Pentateuch for discussion of the matter is a word with two equally plausible meanings that appears in Deuteronomy 6:7, in the following context:

> [4] Listen, Israel, God is our Lord, God is One. [5] Love God your Lord with all your heart, with all your soul, and with all your might. [6] These words which I am commanding you today must remain on your heart. [7] Teach them to your children and speak of them when you are at home, when traveling on the road, when you lie down (*b'shachv'cha*) and when you get up (*u've'cumecha*).

As the context indicates, the word *b'shachv'cha*, "when you lie down," can with equal warrant be translated in two ways. According to Rabbi Eliezer, it means "during the hours when most people retire, in order to sleep." According to Rabban Gamliel, it means "during the hours when most people are asleep." In Rabbi Eliezer's opinion, most people retire by the end of the first of the three (or four) watches into which the night is divided by traditionalists; and so the Shema may be recited only until the end of the first watch. In Rabban Gamliel's opinion (which, he states, the Sages share), most people sleep until the pillar of dawn becomes visible; and so the Shema may be recited until then (though the Sages prefer it be recited before midnight, because thereafter, through fatigue, people may neglect to recite it). Because the two translations are equally plausible, it is not possible to know how late, in, so to speak, God's opinion, which alone constitutes absolute truth, the evening Shema may be recited. That being the case, preeminent traditionalists, acting as a majority, simply choose one of the two equally plausible options, and mandate that it is normative. Because they must do the same thing as regards the other particulars noted, all that can be known to a certainty is that the evening Shema must be recited.

That is absolutely true, because God commanded that it be recited. But precisely how He wants it recited is not certain; indeed, as regards relevant details, it is often, perhaps even typically, not possible to know what He wants.

Because the Mishnah and the Gemara merely discuss law as mandated by the Pentateuch, normative behavior is prescribed not in the Talmud, but in a number of comprehensive codes based upon the Talmud that traditionalists consult as guides to religious law: among others, Mishneh Torah, compiled in the 12th century by Maimonides, and Shulchan Aruch, compiled in the 17th century by Rabbi Joseph Caro, and commented upon in the 20th century by Rabbi Israel Kagan (Chofetz Chaim) in Mishnah Brurah. As a practical matter these codes are indispensable, because they prescribe comprehensively, often in minute detail, precisely how traditionalists must obey God's laws. But as a theological matter they can leave the misleading impression that the laws they mandate are rooted plainly in the Pentateuch, and that how God wants them obeyed is plain. In the example noted, every traditionalist agrees that the evening Shema must be recited, because the Pentateuch—that is to say, God—commanded that it be recited. And it must be recited in a specific manner; but only because a group of preeminent traditionalists has been exclusively authorized to mandate how it must be recited.

And that is the situation as regards the laws discussed below. Chosen at random, and typical of law in the Pentateuch, they demonstrate, as the discussion above of sacred history in the Pentateuch demonstrate, that in many instances, perhaps even typically, absolute truth—by definition, the position that exists in the mind, so to speak, of God—cannot be established; that in consequence, preeminent traditionalists alone authorized by God to do so, formulate norms of behavior without regard to absolute truth; and that those norms are absolutely binding upon traditionalists.

၍

The irreducible uncertainty, in the discussion above, regarding the hour by which the evening Shema must be recited is compounded by irreducible uncertainty regarding whether the third of the three sections into which the Shema is divided must be recited during the evening.

The uncertainty exists because it is not possible to prefer either of two meanings of a phrase, and of a word in a verse, in the Mishnah in Berachot 12b. The phrase and the word in question are italicized below.

> The Exodus from Egypt is to be mentioned [in the shema'] at nighttime. Said R. Eleazar B. Azariah: Behold I am about seventy years old, and I have not been worthy (*v'lo zachiti*) to [find a reason] why the Exodus from Egypt should be mentioned at night-time until Ben Zoma expounded it: For it says: That thou mayest remember the day when thou camest forth out of the land of Egypt all (*kal*) the days of thy life. [Had the text said,] 'the days of thy life' it would have meant [only] the days; but 'all the days of thy life' include the nights as well. The sages, however, say: 'The days of thy life' refers to this world; 'all the days of thy life' is to add the days of the Messiah.

As the footnote below indicates, the phrase in question, *v'lo zachiti*, may with equal warrant be translated in two different ways that necessitate different conclusions. The first translation

> follows *Meiri* and *Rav*, who understand this comment [phrase] in the vein of the Gemara in *Chullin* (31b) . . . *In this matter, R' Nassan prevailed over the Rabbis*. See also *Niddah* 38b. *Rambam*, however, interprets the phrase . . . as meaning, *I did not merit* to find the Scriptural source for the obligation to mention Exodus at night. According to this explanation, all agree that there is such an obligation, in accordance with the opening statement of the Mishnah. The point of contention is merely whether the verse that will

shortly be cited is the source for this obligation (*Tzlach*; see also *Rashba, Ritva, Pnei Yehoshua,* and *Rosh Yosef*).[16]

As can be seen, the first of the two translations above presumes that Ben Zoma (whose position Rabbi Eleazer b. Azaryah appropriates) and the other Sages disagree about a matter of substance: about whether or not the third section of the Shema must be recited in the evening. By contrast, the second translation presumes that Ben Zoma and the Sages agree about the matter of substance, and disagree only about a matter of proof-text: about whether or not a word in a particular verse validates the matter of substance. And because it is not possible to establish what *v'lo zachiti* means, the phrase cannot be used to establish whether or not the third section of the Shema must be recited in the evening.

Neither can the truth of the matter, defined as the position that exists in the mind, so to speak, of God, be established by reference to the word *kal*, if the first translation of the phrase *v'lo zachiti* is preferred. (If the second translation of the phrase is preferred, the matter is moot.) As can be seen, in the Mishnah two irreconcilable opinions regarding the meaning of *kal* appear. In the opinion of Ben Zoma, the word denotes all of a given day, and thus requires that the Shema be recited during the evening as well as during the day. By contrast, in the opinion of the Sages, *kal* denotes the Messianic era, and thus requires that the Shema be recited only during the day. Both opinions are asserted in the Mishnah, rather than argued. (A number of inconclusive arguments and counter-arguments appear in the Gemara.) That being the case, neither opinion can be preferred to the other, and therefore *kal* can no more be referenced than can *v'lo zachiti* to establish the position, so to speak, of God as it relates to the evening Shema.

In Exodus 21:1-11, where the laws that govern acquiring and redeeming male and female Jewish slaves are detailed, it is not possible to know whether a stipulation regarding a male Jewish slave refers to his health or to his marital status; precisely what tool or tools may be used in a ritual performed if a married male Jewish slave declines to be freed from servitude; or to whom, in a particular circumstance, a young female Jewish slave may be sold.

The relevant verses regarding the stipulation are 21:2-3:

---

16 *Talmud Bavli* [The Babylonian Talmud], (New York: 1990-2005), *Tractate Brachot*, 12b, fn. 39.

> [2] If you buy a Jewish slave, he shall serve for six years, but in the seventh year he shall be set free without liability. [3] If he was unmarried when he entered service [*im b'gapo yavo b'gapo yeitzei*]. But if he was a married man his wife shall leave with him.

That 21:3 is contrasting a bachelor and a husband seems evident. But that is not the case, because the first of the two sentences in 21:3 can be translated in two different ways: as in the translation above, but also as "If he came with his body [intact] he leaves with his body [intact]."

Though the second of the translations renders the sentence in question far more literally than does the first, all of the traditionalists concerned with the matter presume that the first translation conveys its plain meaning.

But the Gemara in Kiddushin 20a does not presume it. Instead, it legitimates both translations:

> Our Rabbis taught: *If he comes in by himself* [b'gapo] *he shall go out by himself* [b'gapo]—he comes in with his [whole] body [b'gufo] and goes out with his [whole body]. R. Eliezer b. Jacob said: Having come in single, he goes out single.

The first of the translations above does not presume a bachelor. It presumes, instead, that a master is commanded to compensate his male Jewish slave financially (but not to free him) for injuries he suffers while in servitude. The second of the translations presumes that the subject of the first sentence in 21:3 is a bachelor (and thus that a contrast is presumed in 21:3). But as the Gemara does not prefer either of the translations offered to the other, it is not possible to know what *im b'gapo yavo b'gapo yeitzei* means; that is to say, whether or not Exodus 21:3 discusses a bachelor, or financial compensation for injury suffered in servitude by a male Jewish slave.

The relevant verses regarding the ritual that confirms that a married male Jewish slave declines to be freed are Deuteronomy 15:16-17 (which reprise Exodus 21:5-6):

> [16] If [the slave] likes you and your family, and has it so good with you that he says, "I do not want to leave you," [17] then you must take an awl (*v'lakachta et ha'martzei'a*), and place it through his ear and the door. He will then become your permanent slave.

That the ritual above must be performed with an awl seems evident. But that is not the case, because which of the two Hebrew words above that convey meaning (the word *et* does not) is focused upon determines what tool is required to perform the ritual. And what that tool is cannot be determined.

The two words are analyzed in the Gemara in 21b:

> Our Rabbis taught: '[*With*] *an awl*': I only know [that he can be bored with] an awl. Whence do I know to extend [the law to] a prick, thorn, needle, borer, or stylus? From the verse, *then thou shalt take*, which includes everything that may be taken by hand: this is the opinion of R. Jose son of R. Judah. Rabbi said: Just as an awl is specified, as being of metal, so must everything [used for this purpose] be of metal.

Because Rabbi Jose focuses on the word *v'lakachta*, he concludes that any implement that can be taken into hand can be used in the ritual in question. Because Rabbi focuses on the word *ha'martzei'a*, he concludes that only implements made of metal may be used. Neither sage asserts that the focus of the other, or the conclusion the other draws, is objectionable. And the positions of both are equally plausible. Therefore, it is not possible to know with what implement the ritual in question must be performed.

The relevant verses regarding a young female Jewish slave are Exodus 21:7-8:

> [7] If a man sells his daughter as a maidservant (*l'amah*), she shall not be freed as male servants are released. [8] Her master should provisionally designate her as his bride, and if she is not pleasing to him, he must let her be redeemed. He is considered to have broken faith with her, and he does not have the right to sell her to anyone else *(l'am nochri)*.

That in every instance discussed above the young Jewish woman in question can—indeed, should—be regarded not only as a maidservant but also as a potential bride seems evident.

But that is not the case. In the opinion of the Gemara in 19b, the word *l'amah* in the conditional clause that opens 21:7—"If a man sells his daughter as a maidservant"—legitimates the inference that a father may sell his daughter to a master who is forbidden by Jewish law to marry her, intending, in that circumstance, that she be only a maidservant, not also a potential bride. That established, the question is asked to whom the young Jewish woman who is to serve only as a maidservant may be sold. And that question cannot be answered, because the meaning of *l'amah*, as delimited, cannot be determined.

That the young woman may be sold only as a maidservant to a man who cannot marry her is not in dispute. In the opinion of Hezekiah, because the Writ saith, [*and if a man sell his daughter*] *to be a bondswoman*: sometimes he can sell her to be only a bondswoman. And the Rabbis? How do they utilize this, '*to be a bondswoman*'! – They employ it, even as was taught: '*To be a bondswoman*': this teaches that he can sell her to unfit persons.

Neither is it in dispute that bastards, for example, are "unfit persons" to whom a father may sell his daughter as a maidservant only. But whether certain relatives are also "unfit persons" is a dispute between Rabbi Eliezer and Rabbi Meir (who agrees with the Rabbis) that cannot be resolved, because the disputants assign equally plausible but irreconcilable meanings to *l'amah*.

In the opinion of R. Eliezer, what

> is taught by, '*to be a bondswoman*'? It teaches that he may sell her to [consanguineous] relations . . . . And R. Meir?—[That he can sell her] to unfit persons he deduces from the same verse from which R. Eliezer deduces it; and in the matter of relations he agrees with the Rabbis, who maintain: He may not sell her to relations.

Each of the disputants validates by deduction by referencing his meaning of *l'amah*. But because neither appeal to logic is more plausible than the other, their dispute turns on the irreconcilable meanings they assign to *l'amah*. But because those meanings are equally plausible, the dispute cannot be resolved.

Neither can it be determined to whom the master of the young Jewish woman in question may sell her if, though he should marry her, he declines to do so. In that circumstance he is forbidden to sell her *l'am nochri*. But what those Hebrew words mean cannot be determined. As can be seen, Kaplan translates them as "to anyone else." But as he acknowledges in a footnote, their literal meaning, "to a foreign nation," warrants equally the translation "to a gentile." The first of the translations is preferred by Chinuch (referencing Onkelos), Rashi, Rambam, and Daat Mikrah, among others, the second by Mechilta, Ramban, Ibn Ezra, Sforno, Saadia Gaon, Chizkuni, and Rabbenu Bachya, among others. But because each of the preferences is simply asserted to be the plain meaning of *l'am nochri,* and because both preferences are equally plausible, it is not possible to know whether it is forbidden to sell into servitude the young Jewish woman in question to anyone, or only to gentiles.

In Numbers 29:1, the Jews are commanded to blow a ram's horn on the first day of Rosh Hashanah, the New Year:

> The first day of the seventh month shall be a sacred holiday to you when you may not do any mundane work. It shall be a day of sounding the [ram's] horn (*teru'ah*).

In the Mishnah in Rosh Hashanah 33b, the sequence of the soundings is specified:

> The order of the blasts consists of three sets of three each. The length of a tek'iah is equal to three teru'ahs, and the length of a teru'ah to three yebaboth.

As the Gemara in 33b explains, each set proceeds as follows: tek'iah, teru'ah, tek'iah. However, because an unresolved dispute exists regarding the meaning of teru'ah, it is not possible to know how the command is to be fulfilled. As the uncontested view of Abaya in 33b notes,

> Here there is really a difference of opinion. It is written, *It shall be a day of teru'ah unto you* and we translate [in Aramaic] a day of *yebaba*, and it is written of the mother of Sisera, *Through a window she looked forth* [*va'teyabab*]. One authority thought that this means drawing a long sigh, and the other that it means uttering short piercing cries.

Because the meaning of *teru'ah* cannot be known, the sequence of blasts that fulfills the commandment to blow the shofar on Rosh Hashanah may be tek'iah, followed by a blast (called shevarim) that consists of three fairly long notes signifying a long sigh, followed by another tek'iah, or a blast (called teru'ah) which consists of a number of short notes signifying a piercing cry, followed by another tek'iah. Thus, the sequence of blasts that fulfills the commandment to blow the shofar on Rosh Hashanah cannot be known.

Because it is not possible to prefer either sequence to the other, R. Abbahu suggests in the Gemara in 34a that, as a practical response to the impossibility of knowing what teru'ah means, a combination of both sequences be sounded. In this suggestion R. Awira and Rabina note the same danger, and respond to it by assuming it contains more than is attributed to R. Abbahu. By conflating the suggestion and the assumption, a three-part sequence is prescribed.

In 34a, a difficulty is noted in the sequence prescribed in Caesarea by Abbahu that consists of

> a *tek'iah*, three *shevarim*, a *teru'ah*, and a *teki'ah*. How can this be justified? If [the sound of *teru'ah*] is a kind of wailing, then there should be *teki'ah*, *teru'ah*, and *teki'ah*, and if it is a kind of groaning, then there should be *teki'ah*, three *shevarim*, and *teki'ah*?—He was in doubt whether it [*teru'ah*] was a kind of wailing or a kind of groaning.

This sequence satisfies neither R. Awira nor Rabina, because it entails the danger of a *hefsek*, an interruption prohibited in the fulfillment of a commandment. As they suppose R. Abbahu was aware of this danger, they assume, in 34a, that he must have said more than the Gemara records:

> R. Awira strongly demurred against this procedure. Perhaps it [teru'ah] is a kind of wailing, and the three shevarim make an interruption between the teru'ah and the [first] teki'ah?—We assume that he afterwards blows teki'ah, teru'ah, teki'ah. Rabina strongly demurred against this, saying, Perhaps it is a kind of sighing and the teru'ah makes an interruption between the shevarim and the [second] teki'ah?—We suppose that he afterwards blows teki'ah, shevarim, teki'ah. What then is the point of R. Abbahu's regulation? If it is a groaning sound, it has already been made, and if it is a wailing sound it has already been made?—He was in doubt whether it does not include both groaning and wailing. If so, the reverse should also be carried out, namely, teki'ah, teru'ah, three shevarim, tekiah, since perhaps it is wailing and groaning?—Ordinarily when a man has pain, he first groans and then wails.

Abbahu's suggestion, and the demurrals and presumptions of R. Awira and Rabina, considered together, the sequence teki'ah, shevarim-teru'ah; teki'ah, shevarim, teki'ah; teki'ah, teru'ah, teki'ah is a plausible option. But because it is not possible to know if that sequence reflects the will, so to speak, of God, it is not possible to know how the shofar must be blown on Rosh Hashanah. That is to say, because Abaye asserts correctly that an irresolvable difference of opinion exists regarding the meaning of teru'ah, it cannot be known where the blasts that fulfill the commandment are contained, because if they are contained in any of the three sequences, the other two are irrelevant to the fulfillment of the commandment. If, that is to say, teru'ah means shevarim, the sequences that contain shevarim-tru'ah and tru'ah are irrelevant; and so on. And thus, whatever sequence is codified cannot contain only the mandated blasts. Somewhere, they are sounded, and the commandment is fulfilled; but precisely where, cannot be known.

Reason and Mystery in the Pentateuch

The commandment that Jewish men wear phylacteries is contained in four sections in the Pentateuch: in Exodus 13:2-10 and 13:11-16, and in Deuteronomy 6:4-9 and 11:13-21. In the first of those sections, in Exodus 13:9, God commands that "[a certain set of words] must also be a sign on your arm and a reminder in the center of your head." As can be seen, about how the command must be fulfilled almost nothing is said. The same is true as regards the other three sections noted. The Oral Law, by contrast, mandates numerous details; and because many of them are Laws Received by Moses at Mount Sinai, their authority is, as noted, identical to the authority of the Written Law. But as regards many other details, almost nothing can be known to a certainty. For example, the phylacteries worn on the head must contain only the four sections from the Pentateuch noted above. But the sequence in which the sections must be inserted into the phylacteries cannot be determined, because neither the Written Law nor the Oral Law stipulates what the correct sequence is, and preeminent traditionalists validate equally two sequences, and thus, in effect, two sets of phylacteries. Because in consequence it cannot be known which of the two sets fulfills the commandment, it can be fulfilled to a certainty only if both sets of phylacteries are worn (either at the same time, or seriatim). Because preeminent traditionalists approve of, but do not mandate, wearing both sets, those Jews who wear only one set cannot know if they have fulfilled their obligation to pray with phylacteries. And those who wear both sets cannot know when they have fulfilled the obligation.

Exodus 13:16 mandates that a certain set of words "shall [also] be a sign on your arm and an insignia in the center of your head." In Deuteronomy 6:8 the mandate is to "bind [these words] as a sign on your hand, and let them be an emblem in the center of your head." And in Deuteronomy 11:18, it is to "bind them as a sign on your arm, and let them be an insignia in the center of your head." As can be seen, none of these verses says anything more specific than does Exodus 13:9 about how the command regarding phylacteries must be fulfilled.

By contrast, regarding numerous relevant matters the Oral Law is very specific. As Chinuch, for example, notes in his discussion of Commandment 421,

> Among the laws of the precept there is what the Sages of blessed memory taught: that there are ten things [required] about *t'fillin*, both of the hand and of the head, all being law [given orally] to Moses at Sinai; and if a person alters any of them all, the *t'fillin* are

> disqualified. Two of them concern their writing, and eight concern their enclosure and the tying of their straps. These are the two about their writing: that they [the Scriptural sections] are to be written with ink, and are to be written on parchment. And these are the eight about their enclosures ....[17]

As the two matters concerning the writing in the phylacteries indicate, and as the eight matters not quoted confirm, the Oral Law is sometimes very specific indeed; and especially when its mandates are drawn from Laws Received by Moses at Mount Sinai, specific knowledge of how to fulfill God's command can be established.

Sometimes, however, as in the matter noted, of the sequence in which the four sections of the Pentateuch must be positioned in the phylactery worn on the head, the Oral Law is not at all specific; indeed, it is silent. In that circumstance, preeminent traditionalists must mandate law. And if the grounds on which it favors either of two equally plausible options cannot be understood, knowledge to a certainty regarding the matter cannot be established.

The options regarding the sequence of the four sections are specified in two irreconcilable interpretations of the following mandate in the Gemara in Menachos 34b:

> Our Rabbis taught: What is the order [of the four Scriptural portions in the head-*tefillah*]? '*Sanctify unto Me*' and '*And it shall be when the Lord shall bring thee*' are on the right, while '*Hear*' and '*And it shall come to pass if you harken diligently*' are on the left.

According to Rashi, who references Mechilta, because 34a lists the four scriptural sections in the order in which they appear in the Pentateuch, they must be inserted in that order into the four compartments of the head-*tefillin*, from right to left, as follows: (a) Exodus 13:2-10, the section that begins with '*Sanctify unto Me*'; (b) Exodus 13:11-16, the section that begins with '*And it shall be when the Lord shall bring thee*'; (c) Deuteronomy 6:4-9, the section begins with '*Hear*'; and (d) Deuteronomy 11:13-21, the section that begins with '*And it shall come to pass if you harken diligently*.' According, however, to Rabbenu Tam, in Tosfos 34b, the sections must be inserted in the following order: (a),(b),(d),(c).

The interpretation of Rashi seems to rest, not on intellectual grounds, but on Mechilta's seeming conviction that, as regards the four sections of the Pentateuch, first mentioned must mean first inserted, and so on;

---

17. *Sefer Hachinuch* (New York: 1991), vol. 4, p. 273.

whereas the interpretation of Rabbenu Tam, adducing support from Rabbi Chai Gaon, proceeds from the observation that the Gemara states not, as it could have done, and as it does elsewhere, in specifying how various items are to be positioned, that the four sections are to be placed in a specific order, but that the first two sections mentioned must appear on the right, and the last two must appear on the left.

Because the positions of Rashi and Rabbenu Tam are equally plausible, it is not possible to know how, or when, the commandment to pray with phylacteries must be fulfilled.

⸻

In Exodus 12:1-13, the Jews were commanded to prepare, and to eat in haste, a sacrificial meal sometime before the dawn of the day they left Egypt, disemburdened of slavery. But when they were required to eat the meal—and when therefore they did presumably eat it—cannot be known.

The required time seems to be specified in 21:8-12:

> [8] Eat the [sacrificial] meat during the night, roasted over fire. Eat it with matzoh and bitter herbs. [9] Do not eat it raw or cooked in water, but only roasted over fire, including its head, its legs, and its internal organs. [10] Do not leave any of it over until morning. Anything that is left over until morning must be burned in fire. [11] You must eat it with your waist belted, your shoes on your feet, and your staff in your hand, and you must eat it in haste (*b'chi'pazon*). It is the Passover offering to God. [12] I will pass over Egypt on that night, and I will kill every first-born in Egypt, man and beast. I will perform acts of judgment against all the gods of Egypt. I [alone] am God.

As can be seen, the Jews were required to do nothing during the night their servitude to Egypt ended but to prepare a minutely detailed sacrificial meal, and to eat it in haste (*b'chi'pazon*). But precisely when they were required to hasten cannot be known, because a dispute in Berachot 9a cannot be resolved.

The dispute is concerned with an apparent contradiction between a Mishnah in Berachot 2a and a Baraita in 9a that the Gemara references while analyzing the Mishnah: that the Mishnah does not include the sacrificial Pascal meal among the meals that may be eaten only until dawn, whereas the Baraita does. But the contradiction does not exist, because the Mishnah reflects the position of Rabbi Elazar ben Azaryah, whereas the Baraita reflects that of Rabbi Akiva. But because the positions are equally plausible, and therefore the dispute between them cannot be resolved, until what hour the Jews were permitted to eat the Pascal meal—until what hour therefore they presumably did eat it—cannot be known.

The dispute cannot be resolved because their positions reflect equally plausible interpretations of when the time of haste (*b'chi'pazon*) occurred:

> THE BURNING OF THE FAT, etc. But [the Mishnah] does not mention the eating of the Passover offering. This could point to a contradiction [with the following Baraitha]: The duty of the recital of the *Shema* in the evening, and of the *Hallel* on the night of the Passover, and of the eating of the Passover sacrifice can be performed until the break of dawn. R. Joseph says: There is no contradiction. One statement [the Mishnah] conforms with the view of Rabbi Eleazar b. Azariah, and the other with the view of Rabbi Akiba. For it has been taught: *And they shall eat the flesh in that night*. R. Eleazar b. Azariah says, Here it is said: '*in that night*', and further on it is said: *For I will go through the land of Egypt in that night*. Just as the latter verse means until midnight, so also here it means until midnight. R. Akiba said to him: But it also said: *You shall eat it in haste*, which means: until the time of haste. [Until the break of dawn]

From the use in the Pentateuch of the same language—"in that night"—to describe God's onslaught—at midnight—against the first-born of the Egyptians and His commandment that Jews eat the Pascal meal Rabbi Elazar ben Azaryah concludes plausibly that *b'chi'pazon* means midnight, when the Egyptians, devastated, implored the Jews to leave in haste. But from the fact that the Jews left in the morning Rabbi Akiva concludes, as plausibly, that *b'chi'pazon* means at dawn, when the Jews hastened to leave. In consequence, until what hour the Jews were permitted to eat in haste the Pascal meal, and therefore did eat it, cannot be known.

༶

In Leviticus 21:1-4, the conditions under which, if a wife of a priest dies, he must become ritually unclean for her are discussed. But that is the case only if verses 21:1-4 do discuss a priest's wife. Whether or not they do depends on how a phrase in 24:2 is interpreted, and how a word in 24:4 is translated. And because it is not possible to prefer either of two equally plausible traditionalist interpretations in 24:2 to the other, or either of two equally plausible traditionalist translations in 24:4 to the other, it is not possible to know how, as regards ritual defilement, a priest must act when his wife dies.

Kaplan renders 21:1-4 as follows:

> [1] God told Moses to declare the following to Aaron's descendants, the priests: Let no priest defile himself [by contact with] the dead among his people, [2] except for such close blood relatives (*she'eiro ha'carov eilav*) as his mother, father, son, daughter, or brother. [3] He may also allow himself to become ritually unclean for his [deceased] virgin sister, who is [also] close to him as long as she is not married. [4] [However,] a husband (*baal*) may not defile himself for his [dead] wife if she is legally unfit for him.

In this rendering, the italicized Hebrew phrase in 24:2, *she'eiro ha'carov eilav*, does not mention a wife. Therefore, a priest is commanded to defile himself ritually for a wife who is legally fit for him only in 21:4, and only by inference from the assertion in 21:4 that he must not defile himself for a wife who is not legally fit for him. (A priest may not marry a divorced woman, and a High Priest may marry only a virgin.) But the inference is valid only if the italicized Hebrew word in 24:4, *baal*, must be translated as "husband." It may, however, with equal warrant be translated as "a distinguished person." And if that translation is preferred, the wives of priests are nowhere mentioned in Leviticus 24:1-4, and thus priests are not commanded in 24:1-4 to become ritually impure for their wives, whether they are legally fit for them, or not.

(Wives are nowhere mentioned in Ezekiel 44:25, whose list of relatives for whom a priest must defile himself ritually is identical to the list above.)

In Sifra to 24:4, *she'eiro ha'carov eilav* is interpreted as referring to a wife, and therefore requires that 24:2 be rendered as follows:

> [2] except for his wife, his mother, father, son, daughter or brother.

This interpretation is based on Sifra's rendering of *she'eiro* in 24:2 as "the person closest to him," which it interprets to mean "his wife."

Traditionalism prefers the interpretation of Sifra. It prefers, that is, to suppose, not that verses 24:1-4 nowhere discuss the wives of priests, or two classes of wives, those legally fit, and those legally unfit, for them, or that both classes are mentioned only in 24:4, the first class only by inference; but that they are mentioned twice: the first class in 24:2, the second in 24:4; in consequence to assert when mandating law, that *baal* means not "a distinguished person," but a husband; and therefore to rule that a priest must defile himself ritually for a wife who is legally fit for him, but not for a wife who is legally unfit for him.

Because the two interpretations of the phrase noted, and the two translations of the word noted, are equally plausible, because Sifra is neither Written Law nor Oral Law, and its authority is therefore not absolute, and because in consequence a mandate based on the interpretation and translation rejected, as a practical matter, by preeminent traditionalists would be as plausible as a mandate declared normative by other preeminent traditionalists, it is not possible to know how, as regards ritual defilement, a priest must conduct himself when his wife dies.

⁓

Beneath a dispute in the Gemara in Pesachim 21b that only appears to have normative consequences, a dispute that does have such consequences exists; a dispute that cannot be resolved.

The apparent dispute, between Rabbi Hezekiah and Rabbi Abash, about whether or not a Jew may derive benefit from *chametz* (food that must not be eaten during Passover) in his possession during Passover, is based upon the following commandment in the closing sentence in Exodus 13:3:

> [3] Moses said to the people: Remember this day as [the time] you left Egypt, the place of slavery, when God brought you out of here with a show of force. No leaven [*chametz*] may be eaten (*yei'acheil*).

The apparent dispute is between Rabbi Hezekiah and Rabbi Abbahu:

> Hezekiah said: How do we know that leaven during Passover is forbidden for [general] use? Because it is said, *there shall no leavened bread be eaten*: [meaning,] there shall not be in it permission [i.e., the right] of eating. [Thus] the reason is because the Divine Law wrote, '*there shall no leavened bread be eaten*'; but if '*shall not be eaten*' were not written, I would say, prohibition of eating is implied, [but] of benefit is not implied. Now he differs from R. Abash, for R. Abbahu said: Whenever it is said, '*One shall not eat*,' '*thou shalt not eat*,' '*ye shall not eat*,' the prohibitions of eating and benefit [in general] are understood, unless the Writ expressly states [otherwise], as it does in the case of *nebalah*. For it is taught: *Ye shall not eat of [nebalah] anything that dieth of itself; thou mayest give it unto the stranger [ger] that is within thy gates, that he may eat it; or thou mayest sell it unto a foreigner.*

Because, as can be seen, though Rabbi Hezekiah and Rabbi Abbayu disagree about the equally plausible sources in the Pentateuch that legitimate their pronouncements, the pronouncements themselves are identical, and thus no substantive dispute between them exists. Rabbi Hezekiah's pronouncement that benefit may not be derived during Passover from *chametz* is legitimated by his plausible understanding of why the passive voice of the verb, *yei'acheil*, "to eat." is used, rather than the active voice, whereas Abbahu's pronouncement is legitimated by his equally plausible assertion that, unless otherwise explicitly stipulated (as in the case of *nebalah),* the prohibition against deriving benefit from foods that, for whatever reason, cannot be eaten is always expressed in the active voice of the verb "to eat". But because they disagree only about proof-texts, when mandating normative law they disagree, in the circumstance under discussion, about nothing, because they both rule that a Jew may derive no benefit from *chametz* in his possession during Passover.

In other circumstances, however, substantive disagreement—that is to say, a real dispute—does exist, because in those circumstances the equally plausible sources in the Pentateuch that legitimate equally the positions of Hezekiah and Abbahu positions make it impossible to prefer the position of either disputant to that of the other, because it is not possible, in those circumstances, to know whether the prohibition against deriving benefit from foods that may not be eaten exists only when the passive voice of "to eat" appears in the Pentateuch, or whether the prohibition is (unless otherwise explicitly asserted) expressed in the active voice of the verb.

The most striking example of the relevant concern appears In Leviticus 11:1-47 (and in Deuteronomy 14:3-21), where a comprehensive list is provided of creatures prohibited to Jews as food. A partial survey of the list includes camels, pigs, hares, fish that lack either scales or fins, eagles, ospreys, vultures, ostriches, falcons, owls, bats, most insects, mice, hedgehogs, moles, snails, lizards, ferrets, and small animals that breed on land. When referring to almost all of the creatures on the list the active voice of the verb "to eat" is used. In consequence, as regards almost all of them a question is perforce raised that cannot be answered: whether or not Jews may derive benefit from them. In the opinion of Rabbi Hezekiah, Jews may derive such benefit unless the Pentateuch explicitly says otherwise, whereas in the opinion of Rabbi Abbahu, they may not. And because those opinions are equally plausible, whether or not Jews may enjoy the benefits under discussion cannot be known.

The situation is the same in three examples less striking, but equally inaccessible to understanding to a certainty, in Leviticus 22:12,13, and 16. The first of these verses asserts that "when a priest's daughter marries a non-priest, she may no longer eat the sacred elevated gift." The second asserts that "no non-priest may eat [the elevated gift]." The third asserts that if non-priests "eat of the sacred offerings, they will bear the guilt of sin, since I am God [and] it is I who make [these offerings] holy." In each of the three assertions, the active voice of the verb "to eat" is used. In consequence, the question raised above is raised again, three times, and again cannot be answered. May the priest's daughter in 22:12 benefit from the food she must not eat? May the non-priest in 22:3 benefit from the food he must not eat? If he does in 22:6 benefit from it, does he bear the guilt of any sin? The incompatible answers to these questions are determined as they are above, in the discussion of creatures prohibited to Jews as food; and the questions here can no more be answered than can the question above.

❦

Though the Torah deplores divorce, it is sanctioned by both the Written Law and the Oral Law. But from neither source can it be established when divorce should be granted.

According to the Gemara in Sanhedrin 22a, in his old age King David violated the law of *yichud*, which prohibits a man from being alone with a woman other than his wife, by permitting the beautiful young Abishag to share his bed; but he refused her demand that he marry her, because that would have required him to divorce one of his eighteen wives, the maximum number permitted to him as a king. Of David's refusal

> R. Shaman b. Abba said: come and see with what great reluctance is divorce granted. King David was permitted *yichud* [with Abishag], yet not divorce [one of his wives].

At the divorce of a first wife in particular, the bride of a man's youth, R. Eliezer adds, "the very altar [in the Temple] sheds tears."

Nonetheless, in Deuteronomy 24:1-4 divorce is sanctioned:

> [1] When a man marries a woman or possesses her, if she is displeasing to him [or] if he has evidence of sexual misconduct (*ervat davar*) on her part, he shall write her a bill of divorce and place it in her hand, thus releasing her from his household.

As Kaplan's translation correctly asserts, a man may divorce his wife for either of two clearly distinguished reasons: because she displeases him in some apparently minor way not specified, or because she misbehaved sexually. But, as the translation does not indicate, the two reasons are contained, not in the two relevant phrases in 24:1, but in the single phrase *ervat davar*, which can with equal warrant mean either reason. In consequence, a translation of 24:1 more literal than Kaplan's would read:

> When a man marries a woman or possesses her, if she is displeasing to him because of *ervat davar*—that is to say, either because some relatively minor aspect of her behavior displeases him, or because she displeases him by misbehaving sexually—he shall write her a bill of divorce and place it is her hand, releasing her from his household.

And the more literal translation forces the conclusion that the meaning of *ervat davar* cannot be determined.

That is the conclusion drawn by the Gemara in Gittin 90a, after it records the dispute between the School of Shamai and the School of Hillel (supported by Rabbi Akiva) regarding *ervat davar*.

> Beth Shammai say: A man should not divorce his wife unless he has found her guilty of some unseemly conduct, as it says, because he has found some unseemly thing (*ervat davar*) in her. Beth Hillel, however, say [that he may divorce her] even if she has merely spoilt his food, since it says, because he has found some unseemly thing (*ervat davar*) in her. R. Akiba says [he may divorce her] even if he finds another woman more beautiful than she is.

As can be seen, both schools base their positions on the same phrase, *ervat davar*. Each school supports its position by interpreting differently the two words of the phrase, and its syntax. And the School of Hillel concedes that the phrase "can be taken either way": that is to say, that it is not possible to determine what the phrase means. That being the case, the circumstances that legitimate divorce cannot be known.

⸙

The process by which a husband is punished for defaming his chaste wife by fabricating against her a charge of adultery seems unambiguous. But because a crucial word that appears four times in the relevant section of the Pentateuch can be understood with equal warrant in two ways, it is not possible to determine how the process must unfold.

The relevant section, Deuteronomy 22:13-19, details the process as follows:

> [13] [This is the law in a case] where a man marries a woman, cohabits with her, and then finds himself hating her. [14] He therefore invents charges against her, framing her and saying, "I have married this woman and have consummated the marriage. But I have found evidence that she has not been faithful." (*lo matzati ba b'tu*lim) [15] The girl's father and mother, however, then obtain evidence of their daughter's virtue, (*v'hotzi'u b'tulei ha'naarah*) and present it to the elders in court. [16] The girl's father shall then declare to the elders, "I have given my daughter to this man as a wife, but he has grown to hate her. [17] He has therefore invented charges against her, and claims that he has evidence that she has not been faithful to him (*lo matzati b'vitchah b'tu*lim). But here is evidence of my daughter's virtue" (*v'eileh b'tulei viti*). With that, [the girl's parents] shall present their case before the city elders. [18] The city elders shall then take the man and flog him. [19] They shall fine him 100 [shekels] of silver [as a penalty] for defaming an Israelite virgin, and give it to the girl's father. [The man] must then keep [the girl] as his wife, and may not send her away as long as he lives.

As the italicized phrases indicate, the crucial word in the section above, that appears in two grammatical forms *b'tulim*, and *b'tulei*, means *virginity*; and thus, each of the four italicized phrases means *tokens of virginity*.

But because the crucial word can be interpreted with equal warrant in two ways, and because in consequence the meaning of *tokens of virginity* cannot be known, it is not possible to know how to proceed against the defaming husband.

Specifically, the incompatibility of the opinions, in the Gemara in Ketubot 46a, of Rabbi Eliezer ben Jacob and other rabbis, makes it impossible to identify two important details of the process by which the elders are commanded to deal with the husband.

The first detail concerns the punishment to which the husband is subject; apparently, but not in fact, a clear matter. To Rabbi Eliezer it seems evident that the penalties mandated in 22:18-19—that the husband be flogged and fined 100 shekels of silver—are imposed only if, as 21:13-14 seem clearly to assert, the marriage has been consummated. But the other Rabbis argue that they are imposed whether or not it has been consummated:

> If it was ascertained that the evil name had no foundation in fact, the husband is flogged and he must also pay a hundred *sela* irrespective of whether he had intercourse [with her]. R. Eliezer b. Jacob said: These penalties apply only where he had intercourse [with her]. According to R. Eliezer b. Jacob one can well understand why Scripture used the expressions, '*And go in unto her*' and *And 'when I came nigh to her*,' but according to the Rabbis what [could be the meaning of] '*And go in unto her*' and '*When I come nigh unto her*'? [The Rabbis reply,] '*And go in unto her*' with *wanton charges*, and '*When I came nigh to her*' with *words*.

As can be seen, in Rabbi Eliezer's opinion, verses 22:13-14 beyond doubt assert that sexual intercourse occurred, and that only in that circumstance is the husband punished. By contrast, in the opinion of the other Rabbis, because the apparent references to sexual intercourse are metaphorical, they are not relevant to whether or not punishment is mandated. And the Gemara declines to prefer either opinion to the other.

The second detail concerns the meaning of the phrase *tokens of virginity*. In the opinion of Rabbi Eliezer, it means literal tokens. In the opinion of the other Rabbis, by contrast, it means witnesses.

> According to R. Eliezer b. Jacob one can well see why Scripture used the expression, '*I found not in thy daughter the tokens of virginity*', but according to the Rabbis what [could be the sense of the expression] '*I found not in thy daughter the tokens of virginity*'?—[The Rabbis reply,] *I found not for thy daughter* witnesses to establish her claim to *tokens of virginity*. It was quite correct for Scripture, according to R. Eliezer b. Jacob to state, *And yet these are tokens of my daughter's virginity*, but according to the Rabbis what could be the sense of [the expression,] '*And yet these are the tokens of my daughter's virginity*'?—[The Rabbis reply,] *And yet these are* the witnesses who establish *the tokens of my daughter's virginity*. One can well understand according to R. Eliezer b. Jacob why Scripture wrote, *And they shall spread the garment*; but according to the Rabbis what [could be the sense of the instruction,] *And they shall spread the garment*?—R. Abbahu replied: They explain [the charge] which he submitted against her; as it was taught: '*And they shall spread the garment*' teaches that the witnesses of one party and those of the other party come, and the matter is made as clear as a new garment. R. Eliezer b. Jacob said: The words are to taken in their literal sense. [They must produce] the actual garment.

(In Mechilta, Rabbi Ishmael, commenting on Exodus 21:19, sides with the other Rabbis.)

As can be seen, *tokens of virginity* can with equal warrant refer either to the blood on the bed-sheet in the bridal chamber that testifies the bride was a virgin on her wedding night or to witnesses who testify that she was a virgin.

Both details thus force the conclusion that the process by which the defaming husband of a chaste wife must be punished cannot be precisely known, because whether punishment depends on whether the marriage is consummated, and whether a bed-sheet or witnesses must vouch for the virginity of the bride on her wedding night, cannot be known.

⁓

In Exodus 22:6-8, the liability a guardian incurs when valuables entrusted to him are stolen is stipulated. But the apparent clarity of the stipulation is obscured by two phrases in italics below that create irresolvable uncertainty regarding when the guardian incurs liability:

> [6] If one person gives another money or articles to watch, and they are stolen from the house of the person [keeping them], then if the thief is found, [the thief] must make [the usual] double restitution. [7] If the thief is not found, the owner of the house shall be brought to the courts, [where he must swear] that he did not lay a hand on his neighbor's property. (*im lo shalach yado bimlechet rei'eihu.* [8] In every case of dishonesty, (*al kal d'var pesha*) whether it involves an ox, a donkey, a sheep, a garment, or anything else that was [allegedly] lost, and [witnesses] testify that it was seen, both parties' claims must be brought to the courts. The person whom the courts declare guilty must then make double restitution to the other.

The meaning of the first of the phrases—*if the guardian has not used the valuables for his own benefit*—is clear. The meaning of the second, however, is not clear. It can be translated in a number of ways indicated in the following footnote by Kaplan:

> **22:8 In every case** . . .(following Rashi; *Yad, Genevah* 4:1). Or, "In every case of liability" (*Targum*; Rashbam); or, In every case of negligence" (*Bava Kama* 107B; *Targum Yonatan*; Radak, *Sherashim, s.v. Pesha*); or "In every case of denied guilt" (Saadia).

But none of these translations, or Kaplan's, conveys the plain meaning of the first three of the four Hebrew words of the phrase, *al kal d'var*, which the School of Shammai renders as *every word* in its discussion in the Gemara in Baba Metzia 44a of the Mishnah in 43b.

The Mishnah discusses the point at which the guardian in Exodus 22:6-8 who intends to make use of the valuables (the bailment) entrusted to him becomes responsible for them by juxtaposing the contrasting opinions of the School of Shammai and the School of Hillel:

> If a man intends to make use of a bailment: Beth Shammai maintain, he is [forthwith] responsible [for all accidents]; but Beth Hillel rule, he is not responsible until he [actually] makes use thereof, for it is said, [Then the master of the house shall be brought unto the judges, to see] whether he had put his hand unto his neighbor's goods.

As can be seen, the School of Shammai, by referencing *al kal d'var pesha*, which it takes to mean that the guardian has sworn before witnesses—has actually said—*al kal* d'var—that he intends to make use of the valuables for his own benefit, contends that the guardian incurs liability for the valuables entrusted to him the moment he has expressed his intention to use them; whereas the School of Hillel, by referencing *im lo shalach yado bimlechet rei'eihu*, contends that he incurs liability only when he uses them.

That, subtleties of argumentation notwithstanding, the contentions of the School of Hillel and The School of Shammai are, generally speaking, equally plausible, is underscored in the Gemara in Eruvin 13b by R. Abba, who states in the name of Samuel:

> For three years there was a dispute between Beth Shammai and Beth Hillel, the former asserting, 'The *halachah* [law] is in agreement with our views' and the latter contending, 'The *halachah* is in agreement with our views'. Then a *bat kol* [voice from heaven] issued announcing, '[The utterances of] both are the words of the living God, but the *halachah* is in accordance with the rulings of Beth Hillel.' Since, however, 'both are the words of the living God' what was it that entitled Beth Hillel to have the *halachah* fixed in agreement with their rulings?—Because they were kindly and modest, they studied their own rulings and those of Beth Shammai, and were even so [humble] as to mention the actions [words] of Beth Shammai before their own.

Because, as noted, "the words of the living god" cannot mean incompatible interpretations by traditionalists regarding either sacred history or law that reflect truth, defined as interpretations that exist in the mind, so to speak, of God, but must mean incompatible interpretations that are equally plausible, the reference above in effect underscores that, as in general, so in the dispute under discussion, when liability begins for stolen bailments begins cannot be known.

⁓

In Exodus 21:28-32, the law governing the punishment incurred when an ox (or any other bovine) kills a human being is stipulated. But because a clause in italics below that refers to the owner of the ox when a particular circumstance obtains can with equal warrant be interpreted in a number of ways, the legal status of the owner in that circumstance cannot be known.

The verses in Exodus stipulate the following:

> [28] If an ox gores a man or woman, and the [victim] dies, the ox must be stoned to death, and its flesh may not be eaten. *The owner of the ox, however, shall not be punished (u'baal ha'shor naki).* [29] But if the ox was in the habit of goring on previous occasions, and the owner was warned but did not take precautions, then, if it kills a man or woman, the ox must be stoned, and the owner shall also [deserve to] die. [30] Nevertheless, an atonement fine must be imposed on him, and he must pay whatever is imposed on him as redemption for his life. [31] This law also applies if [the ox gores] a minor boy or a minor girl. [32] If the ox gores a male or female slave, [its owner] must give thirty silver shekels to [the slave's] master, and the bull must be stoned.

The verses clearly distinguish two circumstances. In 28, the ox has never attacked anyone, and is therefore referred to as innocuous (*tam*); in the second, 29-32, the ox is known to gore, its owner has been warned to restrain it but has not done so, and therefore the ox—that is to say, its owner—is referred to as having been warned (*mu'ad*).

(By traditionalist consensus, in the second circumstance the owner deserves to be killed by God, but is not liable to capital punishment imposed by a rabbinic court.)

In the first circumstance, because the ox has always been peaceable, why the owner of the ox should not be punished seems so clear that the Mishnah that prompts the discussion in the Gemara does not even mention *u'baal ha'shor naki*. It is, however, discussed at length by Mechilta and by the Gemara, which record a number of equally plausible interpretations of it that, taken together, preclude understanding of what it means.

In the opinion of Rashi and Abarbanel, the clause underscores the contrast between the second circumstance (in which the owner of the ox deserves to die) and the first circumstance (in which he does not deserve to die). In the opinion of Ibn Ezra, the clause underscores that in the first circumstance the owner incurs no liability. In the opinion of Rashbam, it underscores that the owner has not been warned. And in the opinion of Alschich and Daat Mikrah, the owner in the first circumstance has been penalized sufficiently by the loss of his ox.

The Mishnah in Bava Kamma 41a asserts that

> If an ox gores a man and death results, in the case of *mu'ad* there is a liability to pay *kofer* [a fine]. But in the case of *tam*, there is no liability to pay *kofer*.

As can be seen, the Mishnah does not mention the clause *u'baal ha'shor naki*, perhaps because, as do the traditionalists noted, it seems to presume it means simply that the owner in the first circumstance incurs no liability (*kofer*).

By contrast, Mechilta and the Gemara comment on it at length, and understand it in a variety of equally plausible ways.

Mechilta records four different meanings, each of which forestalls a false conclusion that might otherwise be drawn about the liability of the owner of the *tam* ox from a comparison of a variety of circumstances, the first three noted in Exodus 21:28-32, the fourth not.

In the opinion of Rabbi Yehudah ben Bathyra, the clause forestalls the conclusion that just as the owner of the *mu'ad* ox deserves to die, so does the owner of the *tam* ox. In the opinion of Rabbi Simeon ben Azzai, it forestalls the conclusion that the owner of the *tam* ox must pay half of the *kofer* the owner of a *mu'ad* ox must pay. In the opinion of Rabbi Gamaliel, it forestalls the conclusion that the owner of the *tam* ox must pay half of the *kofer* that must be paid by the owner of a *mu'ad* ox that, in Exodus 21:32, kills a slave. In the opinion of Rabbi Akiva, it forestalls the conclusion that the owner of the *tam* ox that causes a woman to miscarry must pay relevant damages.

In the opinion of Rabbi Simeon ben Zoma in the Gemara in Bava Kamma 41a, *u'baal ha'shor naki* is a colloquial expression that means simply that, because the *tam* ox is killed, its owner ceases to derive benefit from it. In 42a, three other opinions are recorded. In the opinion of Rabbi Eliezer, the clause is relevant to one of two situations in which a *tam* ox cannot be killed: when it killed a person in the presence of an insufficient number of witnesses (and its owner cannot therefore be fined); or when it killed a victim it did not intend to kill (a person rather than a beast, a Jew rather than an Egyptian, a viable rather than a non-viable child). In the opinion of Rabbi Jose the Galilean, the clause stipulates that the owner of a *tam* ox that kills an embryo cannot be fined. In the opinion of Rabbi Akiva, the clause implies that the owner of a *tam* ox that kills a slave cannot be fined.

Because the opinions recorded in Mechilta and in the Gemara are equally plausible, it is not possible to know what *u'baal ha'shor naki* means. Therefore the liability of the owner of a peaceable ox that suddenly turns deadly cannot be known.

֍

In Exodus 23:1 a mandate apparently related to slander is issued. But it cannot be determined to whom the mandate is addressed, what the mandate means by slander, and whether it addresses not only slander but also other matters.

Exodus 23:1 consists of the following two sentences:

> Do not accept a false report. *(Lo tisa sheima shav.)* Do not join forces with a wicked person to be a corrupt witness.

In part because the first of the two sentences can be rendered with equal warrant in a number of ways, it is not possible to determine if it is addressed to an individual in any circumstance, to an individual testifying in court, to a judge in court, or to an individual and a judge in court. Nor is it possible to determine what form, or forms, of slander the mandate addresses, or whether it addresses, for example, procedural as well as substantive matters of jurisprudence, some related to other matters as well as to slander.

Mechilta lists four renderings of *lo tisa sheima shav,* without expressing a preference for any of them, or combining any of them. The first is substantive, the other three are procedural; the first three are attributed to unnamed sages, the fourth to Rabbi Eliezer. *Lo tisa sheima shav* may command all individuals in all circumstances not to listen to slander. It may command judges not to listen to one of two litigants if the other is not in court. It may command a litigant not to present his case if his adversary is not in court. Or it may command that an oath administered in court by a judge be responded to with "Amen."

In the Gemara in Sanhedrin 7b, Rabbi Kahana, responding to Rabbi Chanina, asserts that *lo tisa sheimaw shav* refers to the mandate in

Deuteronomy 1:16 to "hear [the causes] between your brethren and judge righteously." It is thus

> a warning to the court not to listen to the claims of a litigant in the absence of his opponent; and to the litigant not to explain his case to the judge before his adversary appears . . . Rabbi Kahana, however, says: We can derive this rule from the verse: *Thou shalt not take up [sisa] a false report* [referring to the judge], which may be read, *tashshi*.

As can be seen, Rabbi Kahana agrees with Rabbi Chanina about the two procedural matters discussed (though Rabbi Chanina does not restrict those matters to cases involving slander). Moreover, Rabbi Kahana rejects Rabbi Chanina's proof-text in favor of Exodus 23:1, because, he argues, *si-saw* strongly connotes the intention on the part of the litigant to entice or to mislead the judge.

In the Gemara in Pesachim 118a, Rabbi Shesheth renders *lo sisa sheima shav* more broadly, as regards the individual, than does Rabbi Kahana, but less broadly, in that he does not reference the judge; and less broadly than does Rabbi Chanina, because he does not reference matters other than slander. Noting that Exodus 22:30, which mandates that flesh torn from a living animal must not be eaten, but may be thrown to dogs, is juxtaposed to Exodus 23:1, Rabbi Shesheth asserts

> on the authority of Rabbi Eleazer ben Azariah: Whoever relates slander, and whoever accepts slander, and whoever gives false testimony against his neighbor, deserves to be cast to dogs, for it is said, *ye shall cast to the dogs,* which is followed by *Thou shalt not take up a false report.*

As can be seen, in the opinion of Rabbi Shesheth, *lo tisa sheima shav* prohibits any individual in any circumstance not only from relating slander, but also from accepting it, and also prohibits slanderous testimony in court. But Rabbi Shesheth focuses exclusively on the individual involved in slander, and references neither judges nor matters other than slander.

In the opinion of Rashi, *lo tisa sheima shav* prohibits an individual in any circumstances from listening to slander, and prohibits a judge from listening to testimony from a litigant when his adversary is not in court. In the opinion of Alschich, the sentence mandates that evil gossip be neither spoken nor listened to. In the opinion of Rashbam, it mandates that judges investigate scrupulously, in all circumstances, the truth of testimony. In the opinion of Chizkuni, it prohibits slanderous speech. Ibn Ezra underscores that such speech emanates from slanderous thought. Chinuch agrees with Rabbi Shesheth as regards the individual, and explains why a judge is prohibited from listening to testimony from a litigant when his adversary is not in court. (The litigant, he argues, will lie.) In the opinion of Daat Mikrah, the sentence mandates that the individual not speak, or accept, slander in any circumstance, or testify falsely in court; and mandates that judges not hear testimony when only one of the litigants concerned is in court.

As can be seen from the range of equally plausible opinions noted regarding *lo tisa sheima shav,* it cannot be known whether the sentence addresses only an individual, in any circumstance, or in litigation, or only a judge, or an individual and a judge; whether the sentence addresses slander in its general form as evil gossip, slanderous speech only, acceptance of such speech only, or both, or only slanderous testimony in court; and whether the sentence addresses only slander, or also matters unrelated to slander. In consequence, it is not possible to know what the sentence means.

⁌

In Numbers 15:38, God mandates that all four-cornered garments worn by Jewish men contain, on each of their corners, a configuration of tassels known as *tzitzit.* But because which of two equally plausible renderings of a clause in the mandate should be preferred cannot be known, how an element of the mandate must be fulfilled cannot be known.

The relevant clause is rendered below in italics:

> God spoke to Moses, telling him to speak to the [male] Israelites *and have them make tassels (v'asu lahem tzitzit)* on the [four] corners of their garments for all generations. They shall include a twist of sky-blue wool in the corner tassels.

Kaplan's rendering of *v'asu lahem* as a reflexive verb—in effect, as *they shall make for themselves*—is plausible. But the verb can with equal warrant be rendered as *they shall make for them,* where *they* denotes unspecified workers, including gentiles, who make the tassels for *them,* the Jewish men. Therefore which rendering should be preferred cannot be known.

In the Gemara in Menachot 42a, Kaplan's rendering is legitimized by the report of Rabbi Judah, who

> stated in the name of Rab, Whence do we know that the tzitzit made by a gentile are invalid? Because it is said, *Speak unto the*

children of Israel and bid them that they make them fringes; the children of Israel shall make [the fringes], but not gentiles!

In 42b, however, the opposite rendering is legitimated:

Rabbi Mordechai said to Rabbi Ashi, You have had it reported so [that fringes made by a gentile are invalid]; but we had it reported thus: Rabbi Judah said in the name of Rab, Whence do we know that tzitzit made by a gentile is valid? Because it is said, *Speak to the children of Israel and bid them that they make fringes;* others may make [the fringes] for them.

Rabbi Judah can have made, in the name of Rab, only one of the equally plausible reports recorded. But because which of them it was cannot be known, whether or not Jewish men fulfill God's mandate by wearing tzitzit made by a gentile cannot be known.

⌒

When troops mustered for a discretionary war (a war not mandated by the Pentateuch) approach a battlefield, various groups of soldiers are commanded, in Deuteronomy 20:5-8, to return home. (In the opinion of some traditionalists, they are permitted to return home.) But because an irresolvable disagreement exists about a phrase in 20:8, it is not possible to determine which soldiers constitute one of the groups.

The command is issued by lower officers, in 20:5-7, to soldiers who have not yet lived in a house they built, or have not yet harvested the first crops they planted, or have not yet married women they were engaged to; and, in 20:8, to one other group, addressed as follows:

[8] The lower officers shall continue speaking to the people and say, "Is there any man among you who is afraid or faint-hearted *(ha'yarei v'rach ha'leivav)*? Let him go home rather than have his cowardliness demoralize his brethren."

Though the italicized phrase seems unlikely to occasion dispute, three equally plausible meanings of it are presented in the Mishnah in Sotah 44a, and in the Gemara in Sotah 44b.

As the Mishnah notes, the dispute is between Rabbi Akiva, Rabbi Jose the Galilean, and Rabbi Jose:

And the officers shall speak further unto the people etc. Rabbi Akiba says, 'fearful and fainthearted' is to be understood literally viz. He is unable to stand in the battle-ranks and see a drawn sword.

> Rabbi Jose the Galilean says: 'fear and faintheartedness' alludes to one who is afraid because of the transgressions he had committed; therefore the Torah connected all these with him that he may return home on their account. Rabbi Jose says: a high priest who married a widow, an ordinary priest who married a divorcee or haluzah, a lay Israelite who married an illegitimate or Nethinah, and the daughter of an Israelite who married an illegitimate or a Nathin—behold such an one is 'fearful and fainthearted'.

It is not clear from the Mishnah whether Rabbi Jose the Galilean and Rabbi Jose exclude from discretionary wars soldiers excluded by Rabbi Akiva, that is, soldiers fearful by nature, or only soldiers rendered fearful by the transgressions they have committed, that is, by conscience. But it is clear that Rabbi Akiva excludes only soldiers fearful by nature, whereas Rabbi Jose the Galilean and Rabbi Jose exclude also (or only) soldiers rendered fearful by conscience; and almost clear that Rabbi Jose the Galilean and Rabbi Jose disagree about which occasions of conscience dictate exclusion. Therefore, because the Gemara delineates clearly three equally plausible positions, it is not possible to know which soldiers should be excluded from discretionary wars.

The Gemara first clarifies the dispute between Rabbi Jose the Galilean and Rabbi Jose, and then the extent to which Rabbi Akiva and Rabbi Jose the Galilean agree.

As regards the first of those matters, the Gemara asks,

> What is the difference between Rabbi Jose and Rabbi Jose the Galilean?—The issue between them is the transgression of a Rabbinical ordinance. With whom does the following reading accord: He who speaks between [donning] one phylactery and the other has committed a transgression and returns home under the war-regulations? With whom [does it accord]? With Rabbi Jose the Galilean.

As can be seen, in the opinion of Rabbi Jose the Galilean, conscience occasioned by transgression of even relatively minor commandments—that is, by commandments mandated by the rabbis (such as those relating to donning phylacteries) rather than directly by the Pentateuch—excludes soldiers from discretionary wars. By implied contrast, in the opinion of Rabbi Jose soldiers are excluded only for conscience occasioned by relatively major transgressions (such as those listed by Rabbi Jose in the Mishnah) dictated directly by the Pentateuch.

As regards the second matter, the Gemara asks,

> Who is the Tanna of the following: Our Rabbis taught: If he heard the sound of trumpets and was terror-stricken, or the crash of shields and was terror-stricken, or [beheld] the brandishing of swords and the urine discharged itself upon his knees, he returns home? With whom [does it accord]? Are we to say that it is with Rabbi Akiba and not Rabbi Jose the Galilean?—In such a circumstance even Rabbi Jose the Galilean admits [that he returns home], because it is written, *Lest his brethren's heart melt at his heart.*

As can be seen, in the opinion of the Gemara, Rabbi Jose the Galilean agrees with Rabbi Akiva that soldiers fearful by nature are excluded from discretionary wars.

In sum, the Gemara delineates three positions: that of Rabbi Akiva, who maintains that only soldiers fearful by nature are excluded from discretionary wars; that of Rabbi Jose the Galilean, who maintains that soldiers fearful by nature and soldiers conscience-stricken by transgressions dictated both directly by the Pentateuch and by the rabbis are excluded; and that of Rabbi Jose, who maintains that soldiers conscience-stricken only by transgressions dictated directly by the Pentateuch are excluded. (Rabbi Jose's position regarding soldiers fearful by nature is not known.) But which of those equally plausible positions reflects the plain meaning of the mandate in the Pentateuch cannot be determined.

That fact is underscored by the variety of opinions regarding *ha'yarei v'rach ha'leivav* advanced by other traditionalists. In the opinion of Rashbam, the phrase refers to soldiers who are fearful of losing the delights mentioned in 20:5-7—their new houses, their first crops, or the women they are engaged to; their lives, mentioned in 20:8; or any other delight not mentioned in 20:5-8. Ramban and Alshich reference only the opinion of Rabbi Akiva. According to Ibn Ezra, *ha'yarei* refers to soldiers who cannot bear to be struck by enemy soldiers, whereas *rach ha'leivav* refers to soldiers who cannot bear to strike enemy soldiers. According to Chizkuni, the reverse is true. Sifri and Rashi seem not to express preferences, but to list several positions. Sifri notes the unattributed position that *ha'yaerei v'rach ha'leivav* refers to soldiers conscience-stricken by unspecified sins they have revealed to no one; the position of Rabbi Akiva; and a position attributed to Rabbi Jose the Galilean that the phrase refers to soldiers forty years old. Rashi references the positions of Rabbi Akiva and of Rabbi Jose the Galilean, but does not reference the position of Rabbi Jose, or discuss the extent to which Rabbi Akiva and Rabbi Jose the Galilean agree.

Because the opinions above are equally plausible, what the words *ha'yarei v'rach ha'leivav* mean cannot be known. In consequence, which soldiers among those who are fearful are excluded from fighting is discretionary wars cannot be known.

⁓

In Numbers 5:13, God begins teaching Moses the law governing a married woman who willingly commits adultery:

> A man may have lain with her carnally, keeping it secret from her husband, and they may have acted secretly so that there could be no witnesses against [the woman]. *The woman was not raped. (v'hi lo nispa-sah.)*

The sentence in italics seems to warrant the inference that if the woman was raped she would not be subject to the law (detailed in 5:13-27) that debars an adulteress from returning home to her husband (and, indeed, condemns her to a gruesome death). A Mishnah in Ketubot 51a that references 5:13 seems to support the inference without reservation. But the discussion of the Mishnah in the Gemara in 51b, by basing two positions about whether a woman who was raped in a specific circumstance can return home to her husband on her reaction to the rape as it occurs makes it impossible to know how such a woman must be treated.

The relevant section of the Mishnah asserts that if the marriage contract (*ketubah*) a husband gave his wife does not contain a key clause, he is nonetheless bound by it, because traditionalism regards it as statutory.

> If he did not write in her favor [the clause] 'If you are taken captive I will ransom you and take you again as my wife'... he is nonetheless liable [to carry out these obligations], because [the clause] is a condition laid down by Beth Din.

Thus, the Mishnah seems to assert unequivocally that a wife who was captured, and presumably raped, returns home with her husband when, as he must, he ransoms her.

In the Gemara, however, the assertion in the Mishnah is questioned (though that fact is not obvious); and two positions regarding the wife in question are presented.

Samuel's father ruled: The wife of an Israelite who has been outraged is forbidden to her husband, since it may be apprehended that the act begun under compulsion may have terminated with her consent. Rab raised an objection against Samuel's Father: [Have we not learned,] If you are taken captive I will ransom you and take you again as my wife? The other [Samuel's Father] remained silent. Rab thereupon applied to Samuel's Father the Scriptural text, *The princes refrained talking and laid their hands on their mouth.* [Job, 29:9] What, however, could he have replied?—[That the law] was relaxed in the case of a captive. According to Samuel's Father's ruling how is it possible to conceive a case of outrage which the All-Merciful deemed to be genuine?—Where, for instance, witnesses testified that she cried from the commencement to the end. [This ruling], however, differs from that of Raba: for Raba laid down: Any woman, the outrage against whom begun under compulsion, though it terminated with her consent, and even if she said, 'Leave him alone', and that if he had not made the attack upon her she would have hired him to do it, is permitted [to her husband]. What is the reason?—He plunged her into an uncontrollable passion.

Because, as a hermeneutic matter, an assertion in a Mishnah in which dispute does not exist cannot be gainsaid by an assertion outside of the Mishnah, the position of Samuel's Father that the woman in question is forbidden to her husband cannot be taken at face value. That is, in effect, what the Gemara says when it objects to his position by noting simply that he seems to be contradicting a Mishnah. Why Samuel's Father does not respond to the Gemara's objection is not clear. Whatever his reason, the Gemara, in effect, responds for him, by asserting that his position must be that, according to the Mishnah, the woman in question is permitted to her husband only in one of two circumstances: either the suspicion merely, but not the presumption, exists that she was raped ("outraged"); or she cried from the beginning to the end of the rape; and that, according to the Mishnah, in all other circumstances she is forbidden to him. Thus, the Gemara contends, in behalf of Samuel's Father, that he agrees with the Mishnah that the woman in question returns home with her husband, but only if one of the two circumstances noted obtains.

By contrast, Raba takes the position that the second of the circumstances is not relevant: that how a woman reacts while she is being raped does not matter to traditionalism, because they consider her to be in the grip of an overwhelming passion, and therefore not responsible for her reactions, however complex or shifting. (About the first of the circumstances noted Raba does not speak.)

Because the positions of Samuel's Father and Raba are equally plausible, it is not possible to know in what circumstances a captured woman raped and ransomed by her husband returns home with him.

～

In Deuteronomy 11:13-14, Moses informs the Jews that, if they obey God's commandments and love Him, He will provide them with abundant harvests:

> [13] If you are careful to pay heed to my commandments, which I am prescribing to you today, and if you love God your Lord with all your heart and soul, [then God has made this promise]: [14] "I will grant the fall and spring rains in your land at their proper time, so that you will have an ample harvest of grain (*v'asafta dganecha*), oil, and wine."

Kaplan's translation of the two Hebrew words in italics obscures a controversy regarding the harvest that cannot be resolved, because the words can be interpreted with equal warrant in two irresolvable ways. Translated literally, they assert that "you will gather in your grain." But that translation makes it impossible to understand who will gather in the grain, the oil, and the wine in question.

In the opinion of R. Chanina bar Pappa in the Gemara in Berachot 35b, an apparent, but not real, contradiction between "you will gather in your grain" and the assertion by God, in Hosea 2:11, that "I will take back my corn in the time" of harvest, asserts, by contrasting the "*you*" in Deuteronomy and the "*I*" in Hosea, that the harvest belongs to the Jews only when they serve God; that when they do not, it belongs to God, not to them. That is to say, only Jews faithful to God are granted the privilege of gathering in their harvests by themselves.

But that privilege seems to conflict with the far greater privilege, enunciated in Joshua 1:8, of learning Torah without intermission: with God's assurance to the faithful that "This book of the law shall not depart from out of thy mouth." In the opinion, however, of R. Ishmael, no conflict exists, because faithful Jews are commanded by *v'asafta dganecha* to interrupt their learning of Torah to gather in their harvests.

In the opinion of R.Simeon b. Yochai, however, *v'asafta dganecha* refers to the situation in which the Jews are not faithful to God because, he argues, the two words must be contrasted to God's assurance, in Isaiah 61:5, that when they are faithful to Him, they will be privileged to learn Torah without intermission, because "strangers shall stand and feed your flocks"; and that, by contrast, when they are not faithful, they will be forced to gather in, not only, as *v'asafta dganecha* predicts, their own harvests, but the harvests of their enemies; as Moses, speaking in God's name, predicts, in Deuteronomy 28:48, "Thou shalt serve thine enemy."

Because the words "and you shall gather in your grain" can with equal warrant be understood in the two ways noted, it is not possible to know whether or not devotion to learning Torah and work should be combined.

In Deuteronomy 17:14-15, God, speaking through Moses, apparently commands that Jews appoint a king. How and when the appointment is to be made, and who is eligible for the appointment, are clear. But God's use of the word in italics below makes it impossible to determine if, in fact, a command has been issued.

> [14] When you come to the land that God your Lord is giving you, so that you have occupied it and settled it, you will eventually say (*v'amarta*), "We would like to appoint a king, just like all the nations around us."[15] You must then appoint the king whom God your Lord will choose. You must appoint a king from among your brethren; you may not appoint a foreigner who is not one of your brethren.

In the Gemara in Sanhedrin 20b R. Jose and R. Nehorai dispute the plain meaning of *v'amarta*. According to R. Jose, when they enter the Holy Land, the Jews are commanded to choose a king, destroy Amalek, and build a Temple; thus, *v'amarta* must mean that they are commanded to say that they want a king. According to R. Nehorai, if, however, when they enter the Holy Land, they murmur disconsolately that they want a king, they are free to appoint one; but *v'amarta* does not command them to do so.

Because the meaning of *v'amarta* cannot be determined, whether a command to appoint a king exists cannot be known.

The Mishnah in Kiddushin 37a mandates a rule, and two exceptions to it: that, the two exceptions aside, commandments associated with the land itself of Israel must be performed only in Israel, whereas commandments not associated with the land itself must be performed wherever a

Jew is living. About the two exceptions consensus exists. But about whether a third exception exists one of the rabbis and his peers disagree. And the disagreement cannot be resolved, because both parties to it invoke a word in the Pentateuch that supports both equally.

The Mishnah mandates the following:

> Every precept which is dependent on the land is practiced only in the land [Palestine], and that which is not dependent on the land is practiced both within and without the land [in the diaspora], except 'orlah' and kil'ayim. R. Eleazer said, chadash too.

As can be seen, R. Eleazer agrees with his peers that orlah and kil'ayim are exceptions to the rule stated, in that both, though dependent upon the land, must be performed wherever Jews live. But R. Eleazer insists, as his peers do not, that chadash also is an exception to the rule, and therefore must also be performed wherever Jews live. Both disputants reference the same word in Leviticus 23:14, at the end of a section, 23:9-14, in which chadash, and its relation to harvest, are defined. And because the word, in italics below, supports both disputants equally, it is not possible to know where chadash must be performed.

In the section in Leviticus,

> [9] God spoke to Moses, telling him to [10] speak to the Israelites and say to them: When you come to the land that I am going to give you, and you reap its harvest, you must bring an omer of your first reaping to the priest. [11] He shall wave it in the motions prescribed for a wave offering to God, so that it will be acceptable for you. The priest shall make this wave offering on the day after the first day of the [Passover] holiday. [12] On the day you make the wave offering of the omer, you shall prepare an unblemished yearling sheep as a burnt offering to God. [13] Its meal offering shall be two-tenths [of an ephah] of wheat meal, mixed with oil, a fire offering to God. Its libation offering shall be one-fourth hin of wine. [14] Until the day that you bring this sacrifice to your God, you may not eat bread, roasted grain or fresh grain. This shall be an eternal law for all generations, no matter where you live (*b'chal moshvoteichem*).

As can be seen, what chadash is, and when, and how, it must be performed, can be determined. But where it must be performed cannot be determined.

Two offerings must be brought on the second day of Passover: first, a wave offering known as the omer, and then a burnt offering. Until that has been done, partaking of the grain harvested—that is to say, of the new grain, or *chadash* (the Hebrew word for anything *new*)—is prohibited.

But where that prohibition applies cannot be determined, because the meaning of *moshvoteichem* cannot be determined. In the opinion of R. Eleazer's peers, the word means "dwellings," but only "dwellings within the Land of Israel"; and more restrictively, dwellings established in viable communities, by each tribe, in its designated area, only after the Land has been conquered. In consequence, only Jews living in the Land of Israel are subject to chadash, and only when specific circumstances obtain. By contrast, in the opinion of R. Eleazer, *moshvoteichem* means "in dwellings anywhere in the world where Jews find themselves." In consequence, all Jews are subject to chadash.

That both meanings are equally plausible is clear from the Gemara in 37a, which juxtaposes them without expressing a preference for either. In the opinion of R. Eleazer's peers,

> *'Dwelling'* implies after taking possession and settling down. Whereon R. Eleazer comes to say that *chadash* too applies both within and without the Land. What is the reason? *'Dwelling'* implies wherever you may be living.

Thus, because the meaning of *moshvoteichem* cannot be known, where chadash must be performed cannot be known.

༄

In two of the places in which the Pentateuch mandates that the Sabbath be observed, an apparently slight difference in grammar precludes understanding of the penalty incurred when it is perforce violated in an unusual circumstance.

In Exodus 31:16, Jews are commanded to "keep the Sabbath (*ha'shabbat*), making it a day of rest for all generations, as an eternal covenant." In Leviticus 19:3, "every person" is commanded to "respect his mother and his father, and keep my Sabbaths(*shabtotie*). I am God your Lord." In the first instance, God speaks of Sabbath in the singular (*ha'shabbat*), whereas in Leviticus 19:3, He speaks of Sabbaths in the plural (*shabtotie*).

Though seemingly slight, the difference in grammar makes it impossible to resolve a disagreement about the penalty incurred by a Jew who inadvertently violates the Sabbath because he has lost track of the days of the week, and therefore does not know which of the days is Sabbath.

The inadvertent violation occurs because "one is travelling on a road and does not know when it is the Sabbath." That circumstance produces in the Gemara in Shabbos 69b an irresolvable disagreement between R. Nachman, speaking for Rabbah b. Abbuha, and R. Nachman Isaac:

> Said R. Nachman in the name of Rabbah b. Abbuha, Two texts are written: *Wherefore the children of Israel shall keep the Sabbath*; and it is written, *and ye shall keep my Sabbaths*. How is this to be explained? '*Wherefore the children of Israel shall keep the Sabbath*' [implies] one observance for many Sabbaths; [whereas] '*and ye shall keep my Sabbaths*' [implies] one observance for each separate Sabbath. R. Nachman b. Isaac demurred: On the contrary, the logic is the reverse; *Wherefore the children of Israel shall keep the Sabbath* [implies] one observance for each separate Sabbath; [whereas] '*and ye shall keep the Sabbaths*' [implies] one observance for many Sabbaths.

As can be seen, the disputants assign to the two texts in question irresolvably different meanings. Neither disputant argues in support of his position; and the Gemara simply lists both positions. In consequence, because it is not possible to know why in the first instance the Sabbath is referred to in the singular, and in the second instance in the plural, it is not possible to know whether a sin offering must be brought for each of the Sabbaths inadvertently violated, or whether a single sin offering must be brought for however many Sabbaths were inadvertently violated.

༄

Exodus 13:3-10 mandates two commandments designed to commemorate the liberation of the Jews from slavery in Egypt. The mandate seems clear; but two of its words preclude understanding of important aspects of it.

The two commandments—the celebration of Passover, and the use of phylacteries—are presented as follows:

> [3] Moses said to the people: Remember this day as [the time] you left Egypt, the place of slavery, when God brought you out of here with a show of force. No leaven may be eaten. [4] You left this day in the month of standing grain. [5] There will come a time when God will bring you to the land of the Canaanites, Hittites, Amorites, Hivites and Yebusites. He swore to your ancestors that He would give it to you—a land flowing with milk and honey. [There too] you will have to keep this service. [6] Eat matzahs for seven days, and make the seventh day a festival to God. [7] Since matzahs must be eaten for [these] seven days, no leaven may be seen in your possession. No leaven may be seen in all your territories. [8] On that day you must tell your child, "It is because of this that God acted for me when I left Egypt." [9] These words must be a sign on your arm and a reminder

in the center of your head. God's Torah will then be on your tongue. It was with a show of strength that God brought you out of Egypt. [10] This law must therefore be kept at its designated time from year to year (*miyamim ya'mima*).

As can be seen, in 13:3-9 the commandments are clearly distinguished: the commandment regarding Passover is presented in 13:3-8, the commandment regarding phylacteries in 13:9. But which of the commandments is referred to in 13:10 cannot be determined, because the meaning of *miyamim ya'mima* cannot be determined.

Literally, the words mean "from day to day." And if, as they can be, they are translated that way, 13:10 reads: "This law must therefore be kept at its designated time from day to day." In that circumstance, "This law" refers not to Passover, but to phylacteries. And if it does, it can mean, as Mechilta notes, apparently with equal warrant, either, or both, of two things: that (in contradistinction, in both meanings, to the commandment regarding mezuzah) the commandment regarding phylacteries is in force only during the day, but not at night; or that it is not in force during Sabbath and during holidays.

But the words may as plausibly mean "from year to year." In that circumstance, they can with equal warrant be interpreted as referring either to phylacteries or to Passover. Apparently comfortable with both translations, Mechilta notes that, according to Beit Hillel, phylacteries must be examined very twelve months – that is to say, "from year to year". (It notes also that, according to Beit Shammai, phylacteries need never be examined.)

According to Rashi, Rashbam, Saadia Gaon and Ibn Ezra, the words *miyamim ya'mima* mean "from year to year", and apply only to Passover.

According to Chizkuni, the words mean "from day to day" and apply only to phylacteries.

The impossibility of determining whether the words *miyamim ya'mima* refer to Passover or to phylacteries is underscored in the Gemara in Menachos 36a, which lists both readings of the words without preferring either. Referencing, in support of one of the readings, a mandate by Rabbah b. R. Huna, noted by R. Jose the Galilean, that phylacteries should not be worn at night, and, in support of the other, a ruling by R. Akiva, the Gemara asks:

> Did not Rabbah b. R. Huna say that if it was doubtful whether darkness had already fallen or not, one should not take them off nor put them on? Now it follows from this that if he were certain that darkness had fallen one would have to take them off!—This was stated

with regard to the eve of Sabbath. But what can be his view? If he holds that the night is a time for *tefilin* then the Sabbath is also a time for *tefilin*, and if, on the other hand, he holds that night is not a time for *tefilin*, then the Sabbath, too, is not a time for *tefilin*, since the same passage which excludes the Sabbath [from the wearing of *tefilin*] also excludes the night. For it was taught: It is written, *And thou shalt observe this ordinance in its season from day to day*. 'Day,' but not night; '*from day*,' but not all days; hence the Sabbaths and the Festivals are excluded. So R. Jose the Galilean; but R. Akiva says, This ordinance refers only to the Passover offering!

Beyond question, in the opinion of Rabbah b. R. Huna the words *mi-yamim ya'mima* mean "from day to day," whereas for R. Akiva they mean "from year to year." And because both readings are equally plausible, it is not possible to know what the words mean. Therefore it is not possible to determine whether, in Exodus 13:10, Passover must be observed, or phylacteries must be worn.

⁓

Deuteronomy 18:5 details what special provisions must be set aside for the priests of the tribe of Levi, and explains why.

> [1] The Levitical priests [and] the entire tribe of Levi shall not have a territorial portion with [the rest of] Israel, and they shall [therefore] eat God's fire offerings and [their] hereditary gifts. [2] Since God shall be their heritage, as He promised them, they shall not have any [territorial] heritage among their brethren. [3] This shall be the law [of what the] priests [receive] from the people: When any ox, sheep or goat is slaughtered as food, you must give the priest the foreleg, the jaw and the maw. [4] You must [also] give him the first portion of your grain, wine and oil, and the first of your shearing (*v'reishit geiz*). [5] This is because God your Lord has chosen him and his descendants out of all your tribes to stand and serve in God's name for all time.

Because the laws above are presented in the context of the Land of Israel, it seems reasonable to suppose that they apply only in the Land of Israel; that, for example, the law regarding the shearing of sheep applies only in Israel. But whether or not that supposition is warranted cannot be known, because which of two irreconcilable and equally plausible opinions obtains cannot be known as regards the opinion of the Mishnah that the law applies in Israel and outside of Israel, or the opinion of Ila'i that it applies only in Israel.

The Mishnah in Chulin 135a begins with the assertion that "[T]he law of the first of the fleece is in force both within the Holy Land and outside it." Rabbi Ili'a, however, asserts, in a Baraisa in the Gemara in 136a-b, that it is in force only in the Land of Israel.

In 136a Rava assumes that the assertion of Rabbi Ila'i is supported by an argument from analogy presented by Rabbi Ili'a, and quoted in 136b, from which Rabbi Ila'i concludes that the laws regarding "the first portion of your grain (*terumah*)" and "the first of your shearing" should be the same:

> But just as *terumah* obtains in the Land [of Israel] only and not outside it so the law of the first of the fleece should obtain in the Land only and not outside it!—R. Jose of Nehar Bil said, it is indeed so; for it has been taught: R. Ila'i says, the law of the priestly dues obtains only in the Land [of Israel]. Likewise R. Ila'I used to say, The law of the first of the fleece obtains only in the Land. What is R. Ila'i's reason?—Raba answered, He drew an analogy by means of the common expression 'giving' from *terumah*: as *terumah* obtains in the Land only and not outside it so the first of the fleece obtains in the Land only and not outside it.

In 136a-b the Gemara raises and responds to seven objections to Rabbi Ili'a's argument from analogy; and on 136b it notes that as a practical matter, "[n]owadays the world has adopted" the view of "R. Ila'i with regard to the first of the fleece."

Though the Mishnah only asserts its position, whereas Rabbi Ili'a argues in behalf of his assertion, traditionalists assume, as a hermeneutic matter, that Rebbe, the redactor of the Mishnah, could have responded to the argument from analogy upon which Rabbi Ili'a's assertion was grounded, and could have provided the grounds of his own assertion. Because that must be regarded as the case, and the two irreconcilable assertions must therefore be regarded as equally plausible, it is not possible to know whether or not the first of the fleece must be given to the priests only in the Land of Israel, or outside of it also.

☙

From a troublesome request in Numbers 32:1-42 a law is derived in the Mishnah in Kiddushin 61a-62a regarding a condition without which stipulation is invalid. But whether or not the condition is relevant to stipulation cannot be determined, because the Gemara in 61a-62a considers equally plausible two irreconcilable opinions regarding the matter presented in the Mishnah.

The request, not to enter the Land of Israel, but to settle in the Gilead area to the east of the Jordan River, is made to Moses by the descendants of Reuben and Gad. In Numbers 32:28-30, Moses consents to the request only if they accept his stipulation that they fight together with the other tribes in the war to conquer the Land of Israel; indeed, to lead the fight. He orders his subordinates so to instruct them:

> [28] Moses then gave instructions to Eleazar the priest, Joshua the son of Nun, and the paternal heads of the Israelite tribes. [29] Moses said to them: "If the entire force of the Gaddites and Reubenites crosses the Jordan to fight with you, then when the land is conquered, you shall give them the Gilead area as their permanent property. [30] But if they do not go as a special force before you, then they shall have their property alongside you in the land of Canaan."

The stipulation occasions a dispute in the Mishnah in 61a between Rabbi Meir and Rabbi Chanina ben Gamliel regarding the nature of stipulation in general:

> R. Meir said: Every stipulation which is not like that of the children of Gad and the children of Reuben is not a [valid] stipulation, because it is written, And Moses said unto them, If the children of Gad and the children of Reuben will pass with you over the Jordan [. . . then ye shall give them the land of Gilead for a possession]. And it is also written, But if they will not pass over with you armed, then they shall have possession with you in the land of Canaan. R. Hanina b. Gamliel maintained: The matter had to be stated, for otherwise they should have no inheritance even in Canaan.

The dispute is about whether or not, to be valid, a stipulation must be stated twice, first in the affirmative, together with its consequences, then in the negative, together with its consequences. In the opinion of Rabbi Meir, in no other circumstance is a stipulation valid. In the opinion of Rabbi Chanina, however, no double statement is necessary to validate a stipulation in the circumstance under discussion, because the negative statement in Numbers 32:30 is strongly implied—indeed, virtually asserted; its function being to preclude the possibility that, if they do not fight with the other tribes, the Gaddites and Reubenites will inherit neither in Gilead nor in Canaan.

But which of those positions should be preferred cannot be known. As the discussion of the Mishnah shows, the Gemara declines to prefer either to the other, because it finds them equally plausible. And thus it strongly implies—indeed, it virtually asserts—that which of them obtains cannot be understood.

The discussion is divided into two sections. In the first section, the Gemara challenges Rabbi Meir, by imagining that he and Rabbi Chaninah disagree with respect to Rabbi Chaninah's assertion in the Mishnah. In the second section, the Gemara presents four challenges to the position of Rabbi Chanina, and supports his position with a reference from the Pentateuch. In neither section is the position of either disputant weakened. And, the reference to Rabbi Chaninah presented, the Gemara ends its discussion by declining to posit further challenges to either disputant; and therefore leaves the dispute perforce unresolved.

In the first section, in 61b, to Rabbi Chaninah's contention in the Mishnah Rabbi Meir could contend, according to the Gemara, that 32:30 could have ended with the clear assertion that, had they not led the army into Canaan, the Gaddites and the Reubenites would have inherited only in Canaan. That contention Rabbi Meir would counter with another, as plausible, whereupon the Gemara presents a Beraita that supports Rabbi Chanina's contention in the Mishnah. In sum, the challenge to Rabbi Meir proves inconclusive.

That is the case also as regards the four challenges that the Gemara poses, in the second section, to the position of Rabbi Chaninah. In each of those challenges, in 61b, the Gemara references language in the Pentateuch that seems to contain stipulations structured as in Rabbi Meir's understanding of the Mishnah, and that therefore undermines the position of Rabbi Chaninah. But the Gemara responds plausibly, in Rabbi Chaninah's behalf, to each of the challenges.

The first challenge references God's admonition to Cain in Genesis 4:10 about the consequences of virtuous and evil action. The second references a stipulation imposed upon Eliezer by Abraham in Genesis 24:37-41 when he sends him to search for a bride for Isaac. The third references God's statement to the Jews in Leviticus 26:3-38 regarding obedience to Him and its consequences, and disobedience and its consequences. The fourth references essentially the same statement in Isaiah 1:19-20. None of the challenges withstands the support the Gemara offers in behalf of Rabbi Chanania.

That support is underscored in 62a by the Gemara's reference, in 62a, in support of Rabbi Chanania's position, to the oath administered in Numbers 5:19 to a woman suspected of adultery.

The discussion by the Gemara of the dispute between Rabbi Meir and Rabbi Chanania constitutes, at the least, an implicit statement that it cannot resolve the dispute, because the positions of the disputants, grounded in the same text in the Pentateuch, are equally plausible, and because therefore the dispute cannot be resolved. It may even constitute a virtually explicit statement to that effect.

↬

In Deuteronomy 14:22-26 the Jews are commanded to consecrate to God a tithe in addition to the tithe commanded in Numbers 18:25-32. Why they must do so is clear. But an aspect of how it must be done cannot be known, because two opinions regarding it, noted in the Gemara in Bava Metzia 47b, are equally plausible.

The commandment is detailed by Moses as follows:

> [22] Take a [second] tithe of all the seed crops that come forth in the field each year. [23] You must eat this before God your Lord in the place that He will choose as dedicated to His name. [There you shall eat] the [second] tithe of your grain, wine and oil, as well as the first-born of your cattle and smaller animals. You will then learn to remain in awe of God your Lord for all time. [24] If the journey is too great for you, and God your Lord has blessed you so that the place that God your Lord has chosen as a site dedicated to His Name is too far for you to carry it there, [25] you may redeem [the tithe] for silver. The silver [you hold] in your hand (*v'tzarta ha'kesef b'yadcha*) must consist of coinage, which you can bring to the place that God your Lord will choose. [26] You may spend your money on anything you desire, whether it be cattle, smaller animals, wine, brandy, or anything else for which you have an urge. Eat it there before God your Lord, so that you and your family will be able to rejoice.

As the Gemara notes, the aspect of the process detailed that cannot be known is occasioned by an irresolvable dispute grounded in the words italicized above and quoted in a Beraita:

> *And thou shalt bind up the money in thine hand;* this is to include everything that can be bound up in one's hand—that is R. Ishmael's view. R. Akiba said: It is to include everything that bears a figure.

Though each of the disputants references the same verse in the Pentateuch to support his position, they focus on different words. Because the conclusion drawn from each of the words is as plausible as that drawn from the other, it is not possible to prefer either position to the other. Therefore it is not possible to know which position obtains.

In the opinion of Rabbi Ishmael, the three Hebrew words considered together support the conclusion that any money derived from the sale of tithes too heavy to carry to a place appointed by God may be converted to food and drink when God's place is reached, because any money can be "wrapped in your hand." In the opinion of Rabbi Akiva, only minted coins may be converted, because the root meaning of the verb *v'tzarta*, which is not "to hold" or "to carry" but "to fashion," supports the conclusion that only coins that have been fashioned by being engraved can be carried to God's place. Because the opinions are equally plausible, it is not possible to know which position obtains.

All of the evidence presented thus far supports the fact central to the present study: that, to a significant extent, perhaps even typically, it is not possible to establish the plain meaning of the text of the Pentateuch, as regards either of its major components, its sacred history, and its codex; that is to say, that to some significant extent, perhaps even typically, a motif of *mysterium* exists in the two major components of the Pentateuch that, to a significant degree, perhaps even typically, precludes understanding.

Evidence that supports the fact exists everywhere in traditionalist commentaries. But nowhere in those commentaries is the fact derived from the evidence. In the present study it is derived. That, and a discussion of the response necessitated by the fact, and of a counter-response that is not (except in one opinion regarding a specific group of laws) interdicted, but that is essentially without value to traditionalism because it focuses on a theological question of no concern to it, constitute the contribution of the present study to traditionalism.

The response necessitated by the fact is the recognition that though in traditionalism virtually no intellectual inquiry is interdicted, access to intellectual certainty is clearly delimited, especially as regards the theological question. Traditionalism permits inquiry into almost everything, even into the mind and the will, so to speak, of God. But it contends, in the opinion of the present study, that inquiry perforce ends, often, perhaps even typically, in conclusions that are plausible, but not true, where truth is defined as the conclusions, however derived, regarding sacred history and the codex in the Pentateuch that exist in the mind, so to speak, of God; and that all such conclusions are valuable, except those grounded in the effort to access the mind and the will, so to speak, of God, a matter that is perforce of no value, and therefore though, except in one important opinion, not interdicted, is perforce futile. Why God commanded His people to study unremittingly and with a profundity of concentration nothing else, traditionalism insists, deserves the only book that He ever wrote, that contains their sacred history and a codex that mandates how they must live, is evident. That a significant, perhaps even pervasive, motif of *mysterium* is embedded in the book that underscores, almost always implicitly, rather than by direct statement, that understanding is often, perhaps even typically, precluded, is not evident. Nor is the fact evident that the effect of the motif is to strengthen traditionalism, by often, perhaps even typically, confronting traditionalists with the insurmountable limitation of certainty as regards insight, speculation, even thought itself.

As has been shown, that limitation exists in matters regarding sacred history and law in the Pentateuch chosen almost at random: for example, against which of his brothers, if against any, Joseph speaks slanderously to their father, Jacob, why only Joseph is called the child of Jacob's old age, why Joseph prophesies, in one of his dreams, that his mother, who is dead, will bow down to him, why Jacob sends Joseph to visit his brothers in Shechem, who the man, or the angel, is—or the angels are—he meets on the way, where Reuben is when his brothers sell Joseph into slavery, to what group of passersby they sell him, why, when his brothers appear before him years later in Egypt, Joseph assumes that accusing them of spying will effect a family reunion in Egypt, why, at Mount Sinai, God instructs Moses to speak both to "the Israelites" and to "the family of Jacob," why He demands that the Jews both "keep my covenant" and "obey me," how the Jews are sanctified during the three days that precede the Revelation, where Moses is located before, while, and after the Revelation occurs, whether God addresses the Ten Pronouncements only to Moses or to all of the Jews, how many of the Pronouncements, if any, the Jews hear, until when they are prohibited from touching Mount Sinai, when, if ever, they are permitted to ascend it, why, after the Revelation, Moses defers obeying God's command to ascend it in order to perform a series of related actions, whether he devises those actions or is commanded by God to perform them, whether he performs them before or after the Revelation, what Vision is experienced by a group of leaders who accompany Moses part-way up the mountain when, the actions completed, he begins his ascent, why the response of the group of leaders to the Vision seems to anger God, whether Moses, or anyone else, knows how much time he will spend on Mount Sinai, and thus when he will descend, what Korach "took" at the outset of his rebellion, who his co-conspirators are, how many of them are Levites, to what tribes the others belong, why, when Moses first hears Korach's complaints, he throws himself "on his face," how many of Korach's cohort Moses addresses, whether, at one point, Moses becomes angry at Korach, at all of the conspirators, or at Dathan and Aviram, how many rebel, why Moses defers God's command, at the beginning of Deuteronomy, to begin teaching and reviewing an array of commandments in order to recount a complicated sequence of memories, whether he devises the sequence, or records a sequence that God dictates, why the sequence is indifferent to chronology, why Moses mistakenly attributes to an event that occurred in the second year after the Exodus the fatal consequence to himself of an act of disobedience he committed thirty-eight years later, why he seems to remember incorrectly important details of a crucial spying mission and of an important judicial innovation, why he berates his audience for transgressions their elders committed, but they did not, whether the "Hear, O Israel," the evening Shema, must be recited before the end of the first of the divisions into which night is divided, or before sunrise, whether a man may fulfill his obligation to count the omer by listening to another man fulfill his obligation by counting it, what sequence of notes fulfills the commandment to hear the shofar blown during Rosh Hashanah, what the sequence is in which four parchments, each containing a section of the Pentateuch, must be inserted into each of four compartments of the phylactery a man must wear on his head when he prays, how, as regards ritual defilement, a priest must mourn the death of his wife, under what conditions a man may divorce his wife, how a husband who unjustly defames his wife must be punished, when a guardian entrusted with valuables becomes liable for them if they are stolen, what the legal status is of the owner of a bovine that kills a human being, what the law prohibiting slander means, whether a Jew may fulfill the command to wear tzitzit if a non-Jew made them, which soldiers must (or may) return home before a battle begins in a war not mandated by the Pentateuch, when a man must accept the return of a wife who was captured and raped.

Because none of the matters above was discussed completely, and because matters as intriguing and as impervious to understanding pervade the Pentateuch, a comprehensive study of the evidence that supports the fact central to the present study would require an enormous work.

Therefore the evidence presented must suffice, as the study discusses, in closing, what the effect of the fact upon traditionalists must be: to affirm that the only response to the fact consonant with understanding is humility as they confront an insurmountable obstacle to intellectual certainty.

As a theoretical matter, traditionalists understand that that affirmation is the indispensable precondition of productive study of the Torah, because all of them acknowledge and respect *mysterium*. But it is, as a practical matter, a precondition not often articulated, and often, seemingly, honored in passing, if at all. And the disconnect between theory and practice produces the effect noted at the outset of the present study: that though traditionalists affirm, as a theological matter, that the God who Revealed The written Law and the Oral Law—that is to say, the Torah—at Mount Sinai is essentially unknowable, and that in consequence to some significant extent at least, perhaps even typically, the Torah must be unknowable, as regards, most importantly, the sacred history it recounts, and the codex it mandates, nonetheless, given their impressive intellectual dispositions, they tend to presume that they can understand a good deal indeed—a presumption founded in a view of reality antithetical to their own; that in consequence they may understand less than they would if, at the minimum, they were wary of that view of reality; and that therefore they should be, at the minimum, wary of it.

The theoretical affirmation—that is to say, the affirmation independent of the evidence that supports the fact central to the present study—is demanded by the Pentateuch, implicitly and explicitly. The many miracles recounted from the beginning of Genesis to the end of Deuteronomy assert implicitly that God is almost completely mysterious. And His response to Moses, who asks for insight into Him, asserts explicitly that virtually nothing about Him can be known. In Exodus 33:18, Moses asks God to provide "a vision of Your Glory." That is impossible, God explains in 33:20, because a human being "cannot have a vision of Me and still exist." Because Moses is, more impressively than any human being in sacred history, the servant of God, he is granted a unique dispensation; but, as 33:21-23 demonstrate, not even that can yield knowledge of God:

> [21] God then said, "I have a special place where you can stand on the rocky mountain. [22] When My Glory passes by, I will place you in a crevice in the mountain, protecting you with My power

until I pass by. [23] I will then remove My protective power, and you will have a vision of what follows from My existence(*achorei*). My essence itself (*panei*), however, will not be seen.

Whatever is meant by "follows from my existence"—Kaplan's translation, referencing Maimonides, of *achorei*, which means literally "my back"—and of "My essence"—Kaplan's translation of *panei*, which means literally "my face"—not even Moses, it seems, can know anything of God's essence, or have any access, other than what He provides, explicitly and only very infrequently, to the rational process—if, indeed, any such process exists—that occasions the mandates in His codex.

And if Moses cannot attain such knowledge, no one can. No traditionalist disputes that. To the contrary, all of them affirm it.

That almost all of them comment nonetheless upon almost every word in the Pentateuch is laudable, because their collective effort bespeaks their profound devotion to God, and to the only book He ever wrote, primarily for the benefit of His Chosen People, to recount their sacred history, and to mandate the laws that must bind them. But it is laudable only insofar as that devotion is safeguarded by the fact central to the present study: that, often, perhaps even typically, conclusions about sacred history must be regarded as plausible speculation, not as definitive explanations of events; that, often, perhaps even typically, binding laws mandated by preeminent traditionalists in the codex are unrelated to truth, defined as the positions regarding them that exist in, so to speak, the mind of God; and that, except when, as happens only very infrequently, God explains why He mandated a law, all efforts to establish what His reasons are, or even (in one opinion) to think about that matter, though not interdicted, are perforce futile, because they presume, in effect, that human beings can gain access to, so to speak, the mind of God, and therefore in effect to deny, as a view of reality antithetical to their own denies, that He cannot be known.

The essential distinction between traditionalism and the view that is antithetical to it because it denies that *mysterium* exists by asserting axiomatically that the human mind impressive enough and well enough disciplined can comprehend all of reality is underscored by one traditionalist opinion regarding the group of laws in the Pentateuch known as *chukim*, laws that God mandated for reasons that cannot be understood, and that, in the opinion referred to, must not even be thought about. As will be seen, that opinion need not, as a theological matter, be accepted; but the fact central to the present study supports it decisively, as regards not only *chukim*, but the codex in general, and undermines decisively the counter-opinion, that God's reasons, so to speak, for mandating not only the *chukim* but the codex in general can be thought about, and in some measure, perhaps even typically, understood.

The opinion appears in the Gemara in Yoma 67b, which decrees that traditionalist Jews taunted for obeying *chukim* must proclaim their fidelity to God even when He commands them to desist from thinking:

> Because Satan and the nations of the world taunt Israel, saying, "What is this commandment? What is the reason for it?" Therefore, the Torah referred to it as *chukah*, a statute. I have decreed it, and you are not permitted to question it (*l'harheir achare'ha*).

The decree, however, is not burdensome, because though nothing in traditionalism asserts that human beings can have access to the mind of God except when He chooses, as He does only very infrequently, to explain Himself, nothing prohibits traditionalists from speculating even about what God was, so to speak, thinking when He mandated the laws in the codex that are not *chukim*; because even whether *chukim* may be thought about—even, indeed, whether they exist—may be thought about, apparently without theological risk, as Maimonides' shifting opinions regarding the matter, discussed below, indicate.

That being the case, that most traditionalists do speculate about the matter is not surprising. "Most authorities" agree

> that there are reasons for all the statues, although we may not always understand them. For discussion of this and related issues see *Sanhedrin* 21b; *Rambam, Moreh Nevuchim* 3:26, 3:31, and 3:48; ibid., *Hil. Teshuvah* 3:4, *Hil. Me'ilah* 8:8, *Hil. Temurah* 4:13 and Hil. Mikvaos 11:12; *Tosafos* to *Gittin* 49b ... with *Maharam*; *Ibn Ezra* to *Exodus* 20:1; *Ramban* to *Leviticus* 18:6 and 19:19 and to *Deuteronomy* 22:6; *Chinuch* 545; *Derashos HaRan* 11; *Akeidah* to *Numbers* 19:1; *Tos. Yom Tov* to *Berachos* 5:3; *Nefesh HaChaim* 1:22; *Sfas Emes, Parashas Mishpatim* 5631; ibid., *Parashas Parah*, 5631; ibid., Parashas Chukas 5632. Regarding the *Azazel* goat in particular, see *Moreh Nevuchim* 3:46; *Ramban* to *Leviticus* 16:8; Meiri, *Chibbur HaTeshuvah* 2:13 p.546-7.[18]

That these traditionalists, and others, should speculate about a matter not interdicted—about what God was, so to speak, thinking when He formulated the mandates that are not *chukim*—may, however, be futile, for

---

18. *Talmud Bavli, Tractate Yoma*, 67b, fn. 29.

either of two reasons: that God may not have been, so to speak, thinking at all; or, even if He was, so to speak, thinking, that, as the present study contends, to a significant degree, perhaps even typically, the book He wrote is impervious to comprehension, especially as regards why He mandated the laws in the codex.

As noted, that a community of traditionalists that has flourished through many centuries and that is preeminent in intellectual acumen should "maintain that there are reasons for all the statues," and should presume that, especially because its aspiration is spiritual illumination, the reasons may eventually yield to the acumen, is not surprising. The aspiration, however, is not supported by the Torah, the book upon which the view of reality of traditionalism is grounded; it is, to the contrary, in the opinion of he present study, often, perhaps even typically, thwarted by the Torah.

The presumption and the aspiration notwithstanding, the Gemara juxtaposes two irreconcilable positions—that the mandates in the codex are expressions of God's intelligence (the Rationalist position) and that they are expressions of His will (the Voluntarist position)—and prefers the second. That is to say, it contrasts the position that the codex contains what God, so to speak, *thought* it should contain and the position that it contained what He, so to speak, *wanted* it to contain, and supports the second rather than the first.

The positions concern a law in Deuteronomy 22:6-7 that is analyzed in the Gemara in Berachot 33b. The law mandates that

> [6] If you come across a bird's nest on any tree or on the ground and it contains baby birds or eggs, then, if the mother is sitting on the chicks or eggs, you must not take the mother along with her young. [7] You must first chase away the mother, and only then may you take the young.

Commenting on the law, the Mishnah asserts that "If one [in praying] says 'May thy [God's] mercies extend to a bird's nest ... he is silenced." the Gemara contrasts two opinions about why the person praying is silenced:

> Two Amorim in the West, R. Jose b. Abin and R. Jose b. Zebida, give different answers; one says it is because he creates jealousy among God's creatures, the other, because he presents the measures taken by the Holy One, blessed be He, as springing from compassion, whereas they are but decrees.

As can be seen, the Gemara rejects the reasons given by both Amorim; not, however, to offer another reason, but to imply strongly that the effort to understand the reasoning that occasioned the mandate is futile, because the mandate is the expression not of, so to speak, God's reason at all, but of, so to speak, His will; in other words that, the practical presumption of traditionalists notwithstanding, the mandate under discussion may bespeak God not as Rationalist, but as Voluntarist; and that that may be the case for the codex in general.

Even if that is not the case—even if the codex bespeaks God's intelligence—the effort to trace His intelligence in the codex is perforce futile in proportion as the thesis of the present study establishes *mysterium* as an important motif in the Pentateuch; and is entirely futile if the motif is, as the study thinks is perhaps the case, pervasive. That is to say, even if God's reasoning, so to speak, underlies all of the laws in the codex, but the language of the Pentateuch, the source of all traditionalist law, often, perhaps even typically, precludes comprehension, whether God is a Voluntarist or a Rationalist is a matter of no significance, whereas the insurmountable obstacle to comprehension created by His use of language throughout the Pentateuch—the obstacle immanent throughout the text—is a matter of pervasive significance.

The conviction that that cannot be the case—that God would not have fashioned in the Pentateuch such an obstacle to thwart the rationalism of traditionalists—is expressed most forcefully by perhaps the most gifted of them, Moses Maimonides, to whom alone traditionalism has for centuries addressed the compliment that *mei moshe y'ad moshe lo kam k'moshe*. (From the time of Moses to the time of Moses Maimonides no traditionalist as impressively rational as Moses appeared.) That conviction is, however, challenged by an esteemed modern traditionalist; a challenge that is especially noteworthy because he is a committed Maimonidean.

Maimonides' conviction shifts in Mishneh Torah, an early work, and stabilizes in Moreh Nevuchim, a late work. In Mishneh Torah, his reaction to the pronouncement in the Gemara in Yoma 67b that human beings are forbidden even to think about why God mandated *chukim* ranges from complete acceptance to complete rejection. In The Guide of the Perplexed, Maimonides' final word on the matter, complete rejection prevails: the conviction that the human mind, impressive enough and well enough disciplined, can (minor details excepted) grasp the meaning not only of almost all of the *chukim*, but of almost all of the God's laws.

As regards the bird's nest in Deuteronomy 22:6-7, discussed above, Maimonides' position in Hilchot Tefilah 9:7 is indistinguishable from that in Yoma 67b:

> One who says in his supplicatory prayers: "May He Who showed mercy on a bird's nest prohibiting the taking of the mother together with the chicks, or the slaughter of an animal and its calf on the same day, also show mercy on us," or [makes other] similar statements should be silenced, because these are God's decrees and not [expressions] of mercy.[19]

Maimonides' position is indistinguishable from Rashi's also in the strongly implied contrast underscored, in Hilchot Me'Ilah 8:8, between those laws that are accessible to human understanding (*mishpatim*) and those that are not (*chukim*). As regards mishpatim,

> It is appropriate for a person to meditate on the judgments (*b'mishpetei*) of the holy Torah and to know their ultimate purpose.[20]

By contrast, no mention is made of meditating upon *chukim*, in order to know why God, so to speak, mandated them; Maimonides' silence as regards that matter strongly implying that such meditation upon *chukim* is interdicted; an implication underscored by the precedence granted to *chukim* over *mishpatim*.

> For through the performance of the decrees (*chukim*) and the judgments (*mishpatim*), the righteous merit the life of the world to come [And between the two of them,] the Torah gave precedence to the commands for the decrees (*chukim*), as [Leviticus 18:5] states: "And which a person will perform and live through them."[21]

In Hilchot Mikveot 11:12, Maimonides asserts that the position in Yoma 67b applies also to immersion in a *mikveh* (a ritual bath), but then undermines that position by thinking about why God mandated the immersion.

The assertion confirms that it is

> a clear and apparent matter that the concepts of purity and impurity are Scriptural decrees. They are not matters determined by a person's understanding and they are included in the category of *chukim*. Similarly, immersion [in a *mikveh* to ascend from] impurity is

---

19 Moses Maimonides, *Mishneh Torah, Hilchot Tefllah II* (New York: 1989), pp.73-74.
20. *Sefer Ha'avodah, Hilchot Me'ilah*, p.898.
21. Ibid., p.900.

> included in the category of *chukim*, because impurity is not mud or filth that can be washed away with water. Instead, [the immersion] is a Scriptural decree and requires the [focusing] the intent of one's heart. Therefore our Sages said: "[When] one immersed, but did not intend to purify himself," it is as if he did not immerse.

The confirmation established, however, Maimonides thinks, though only tentatively and obliquely, about why God mandated the *chok,* by considering its effect.

> Although it [is a Scriptural decree], there is an allusion involved: One who focuses his heart on purifying himself becomes purified once he immerses, even though there was no change in his body. Similarly, one who focuses his heart on purifying his soul from the impurities of the soul, which are wicked thoughts and bad character traits becomes purified when he resolves within his heart to distance himself from such counsel and immerse his soul in the waters of knowledge. And [Ezekiel 36:25] states "I will pour over you pure water and you will be purified from all your impurities and from all your false deities, I will purify you."[22]

In Hilchot Temurah 4:13, Maimonides asserts simultaneously that the position of Yoma 67b applies to specific redemption values, and that thinking, far more explicitly and emphatically than as regards ritual immersion, about why God mandated those values is entirely appropriate.

> Although all the statutes of the Torah are decrees, as we explained in the conclusion of *[Hilchot] Me'ilah*, it is fit to meditate upon them, and wherever it is possible to provide a reason (*ta'am*), one should provide a reason. The Sages of the early generations said that King Solomon understood most of the rationales (*hata'amim*) for all the statutes of the Torah.
>
> It appears to me that the verse [Leviticus 27:10]: "It and the animal to which its holiness will be transferred shall be consecrated" shares a similar [motivating rationale as] the verse [*ibid.*:15]: "If the one who consecrates it shall redeem his house, he shall add a fifth of the money of the redemption valuation to it." [The principle behind these laws is that] the Torah descended to the depths of a person's thoughts and the scope of his evil inclination. For [it is] human nature to tend to increase one's property and attach importance to his money. Even though one made a vow or consecrated something, it is possible that he will reconsider, change

---

22. *Sefer Taharah II, Hilchot Mikveot,* p. 596.

his mind, and redeem it for less than its worth. Hence the Torah states: "If he redeem it for himself, he must add a fifth." Similarly, if he consecrated an animal in a manner that its physical person became consecrated, he might reconsider. [In this instance,] since he cannot redeem it, he will exchange it for a lesser one. If he were given permission to exchange a superior animal for an inferior one, he will exchange an inferior one for a superior one, and claim that it was superior. Therefore, the Torah removed that option, forbidding [all] exchanges and penalized him that if made an exchange, "It and the animal to which its holiness will be transferred shall be consecrated."[23]

In *The Guide of the Perplexed* 3:25-50[24] no shifts in position of the sort noted above in Mishneh Torah regarding Yoma 67b exist, because Maimonides' position has stabilized into the conviction that not only virtually all of the *chukim*, but virtually all of God's commandments, can be understood. Maimonides asserts explicitly that he understands, to a certainty, why God mandated virtually all of the commandments, and explains all but minor details of why He mandated them; and thus asserts, in effect, that (with one possible exception) *chukim* do not exist; and thus that, at least as far as the codex of the Pentateuch is concerned, *mysterium* does not exist.

In 3:25 Maimonides rejects, on theological grounds, the essential tenet of Voluntarism—that the thought and actions of God are governed by will alone—that He simply wills the commandments He mandates—and explains why, to the contrary, He must have reasons for prescribing them. That done, in 3:27-50, he explains why God mandated virtually all of the six hundred and thirteen commandments contained in the Pentateuch.

Two related assertions in 3:26 constitute the preface to 3:27-50: that neither the plain meaning assigned to the Gemara in Yoma 67b by Rashi in his commentary on Numbers 19:2, and by himself in *Mishneh Torah*, nor the meaning both assigned there to *chukim*, is accurate.

In Maimonides' opinion, the relevant assertion in Yoma 67b is not to be taken at face value. It seems to assert that human beings are forbidden even to think about the *chukim*:

> [The Sages], *may their memory be blessed*, make literally the following statement: *Things which I have prescribed for you, about*

---

23. *Mishneh Torah, Sefer Hakorbanot*, pp. 368-370.
24. Moses Maimonides, *The Guide of the Perplexed* (Chicago: 1963), vol. 2, pp. 502-617.

> which you have not the permission to think, which are criticized by Satan and refuted by the Gentiles.

But the plain meaning of the Gemara's assertion is, Maimonides asserts, that the Voluntarists are wrong, because it underscores that the *chukim*

> are not believed by the multitude of the *Sages* to be things for which there is no cause at all and for which one must not seek an end. For this would lead, according to what we have explained, to their being considered as futile actions. On the contrary, the multitude of the *Sages* believe that there is indubitably a cause for them—I mean a useful end—but that it is hidden from us either because of the incapacity of our intellects or the deficiency of our knowledge. Consequently there is, in their opinion, a cause for all the *commandments*; I mean to say that any particular commandment or prohibition has a useful end.[25]

The explanation referred to is Maimonides' rejection of Voluntarism in 3:25. And the ambiguity in "the incapacity of our intellects" is nullified almost immediately by the distinction Maimonides makes between commandments that seem reasonable and those that do not, and thereafter in a detailed discussion regarding the latter that occupies most of the rest of 3:26.

The ambiguity exists in Kapach's Hebrew translation of Maimonides' Aramaic text as well as in Pines' English translation. "[T]he incapacity of our intellects" (*machmat kotzer sichleinu*) may refer to a deficiency of intelligence in particular individuals, or in the human condition. That ambiguity, however, is nullified immediately by the following distinction:

> Those commandments whose utility is clear to the multitude (*ha'mon*) are called *mishpatim* [*judgments*], and those whose utility is not clear to the multitude are called *chuqqim* [*statutes*].

In other words, no obstacle inherent in the human condition prevents human beings intelligent enough and well enough disciplined from understanding, to a certainty, why God mandated, not only virtually all of the *chukim*, but virtually all of the laws in the Pentateuch. And thus, Maimonides asserts, addressing a particular reader, rather than human beings in general, and referencing first Deuteronomy 32:47, and then the gloss upon it in the Jerusalem Talmud, Pe'ah 1, that it is

> no vain thing—*And if it is vain, it is because of you*; meaning that this legislation is not a vain matter without a useful end and that

---

25. Ibid., p. 507.

if it seems to you that this is the case with regard to some of the *commandments*, the deficiency resides in your apprehension.[26]

Only one exception is conceded: "that concerning the *red heifer*."[27] Otherwise, any traditionalist intelligent enough and well enough disciplined may not only think about, so to speak, God's reasons for mandating *chukim*, but may aspire to discover, to a certainty, why He mandated them. And if that is so as regards *chukim*, it must be true as regards the codex in general.

The only limit to the aspiration Maimonides sanctions is discussed in the closing section of 3:26, in the warning that the minor details of all of the commandments—of the *mishpatim* as well as of the *chukim*—of their nature elude comprehension, and that in consequence even thinking about them, though not interdicted, is pathologically foolish. For example:

> The offering of sacrifices has in itself a great and manifest utility, as I shall make clear. But no cause will ever be found for the fact that one particular sacrifice consists in a *lamb* and another in a *ram* and that the number of the victims should be one particular number. Accordingly, in my opinion, all those who occupy themselves with finding causes for something of these particulars are stricken with a prolonged madness in the course of which they do not put an end to an incongruity, but rather increase the number of incongruities.[28]

The limitation above understood, the traditionalist intelligent enough and well enough disciplined may approach even the *chukim* without unwarranted reservations regarding *mysterium*.

That is what Maimonides announces he will do. Supported, he says, by the "constant statements of [the Sages] to the effect that there are causes for all of the commandments," and apparently confident that nothing inherent in the human condition debars him from discovering them,

> I have seen fit to divide the *six hundred and thirteen commandments* into a number of classes, every one of which comprises a number of *commandments* belonging to one kind or akin in meaning. I shall inform you of the cause of every one of these classes, and I shall show their utility about which there can be no doubt and to which there can be no objection. Then I shall return to each of the *commandments* comprised in the class in question and I shall explain to

26. Ibid., p. 507.
27. Ibid.
28. Ibid., p. 509.

you the cause of it, so that only very few *commandments* will remain whose cause has not been clear to me up to now."[29]

The only ambiguity that may exist in the announcement above—regarding whether Maimonides considers the reasons he will assign to each of the commandments speculative or definitive—is nullified implicitly by a statement within the announcement, and explicitly by two unequivocal assertions in its proximity.

The statement—that he will identify reasons "about which there can be no doubt and to which there can be no objection"—reflects Maimonides' apparently unambiguous confidence that his reasons should perforce be regarded as definitive. In 3:28, referring to the *chukim*, he states explicitly that he will present "the correct and demonstrated causes for them all."[30] And in 3:29, he states explicitly that he will "explain the reasons for the commandments that are considered to be without cause" so convincingly that his reader "will know for certain that what I say about the reasons for these laws is correct."[31]

The task regarding God's commandments, and the minor stipulation regarding them, established in 3:25-26, in 3:27-34, Maimonides details the premises that introduce the task, and in 3:35-50 fulfills, in his view, the task, by dividing, not only the *chukim*, but all of the commandments in the Pentateuch, into fourteen classes, and explaining what God's reasons were for mandating virtually all of them.

The explanations are rigorous, lucid, and comprehensive. They are, however, of no value to traditionalism; in the judgment of the present study, because they are grounded, as a matter of intellectual history, in a view of reality antithetical to that of traditionalism, and, far more important, because they are undermined decisively by the thesis of the study: that, as regards not only the codex detailed in the Pentateuch, but also the sacred history it records, such explanations are precluded, except as plausible speculation, by the significant, perhaps even pervasive, motif in the Pentateuch of *mysterium*; and in the judgment of a modern traditionalist, Rabbi Joseph B. Soloveitchik, who notes that "one of the perplexing problems that has confused the finest minds is that of [Maimonides'] rationalization of the commandments" and explains why that is so.

---

29. Ibid., pp. 509-510.
30. Ibid., p. 513.
31. Ibid., p. 518.

Reason and Mystery in the Pentateuch

The difficulties encountered by Maimonides in his attempt to eliminate Saadiah and Bahya's dualism of Rational and Traditional commandments (*shimei'ot* and *sichli'ot*), and to develop an all-embracing interpretation of religious norms are well known. Twenty-five chapters of the *Guide* are devoted exclusively to the solution of this problem. However, Maimonides' attempt at rationalization ... did not succeed in making his interpretation of the commandments prevalent in our world perspective. While we recognize his opinions on more complicated problems such as prophecy, teleology and creation, we completely ignore most of his rational notions regarding the commandments. The reluctance on the part of the Jewish *homo religiosus* to accept Maimonidean rationalistic ideas is not ascribable to any agnostic tendencies, but to the incontrovertible fact that such explanations neither edify nor inspire the religious consciousness. They are essentially, if not entirely, valueless for the religious interests we have most at heart. Maimonides' failure to impress his rationalistic method upon the vivid religious consciousness is to be attributed mainly to the fact that the central theme of the Maimonidean exposition is the causalistic problem. The "how" question, the explanatory quest, and the generic attitude determined Maimonides' doctrine of the commandments. Instead of describing, Maimonides explained; instead of reconstructing, he constructed.[32]

In the opinion of the present study, the judgment above warrants careful attention because its author represents a distinguished intellectual tradition; because it constitutes a judgment not only of Maimonides, but of all efforts by traditionalists to rationalize the commandments mandated by God in the Pentateuch; and because it underscores that, though traditionalists may speculate about any aspect of traditionalism, as regards that matter, nothing, perforce, of value will be discovered. Thus the judgment is entirely correct; except that its response may be questioned to a plausible conjecture that has remained, through more than eight centuries, in dispute.

That the judgment is that of Rabbi Soloveitchik, scion of a family of traditionalists whose devotion to Maimonides is preeminent among traditionalists lends to it such weight as the argument from authority can.

The judgment is especially useful because it obviates discussion of all traditionalists who formulate rationalistic explanations of the commandments in the Pentateuch. All of them do what Maimonides does. None of

---

32. Joseph B. Soloveitchik, *The Halakhic Mind* (New York: 1986), p. 92.

them does it as impressively. Therefore the judgment that pertains to Maimonides pertains also to them.

Because it recognizes that the freedom of inquiry afforded by the judgment to traditionalists is virtually unlimited, it underscores that not even inquiry into God's reasons, so to speak, for mandating the commandments in the Pentateuch is interdicted; stipulating only that such inquiry is perforce "vain" and therefore "essentially, if not entirely, valueless" for productive speculation by traditionalists.

The stipulation is grounded in the judgment that to focus, as Maimonides does, on what God was, so to speak, thinking when He mandated laws, rather than on precisely how to obey His laws, is to court vanity. Why that is so—why the focus on, so to speak, God's intellect or on, so to speak, His will, must produce nothing of value—in the equivalent word of the present study, must prove futile—Rabbi Soloveitchik does not explain. (The present study does, in detail.)

The plausible conjecture summarily rejected by Rabbi Soloveitchik—that Maimonides' effort to rationalize virtually all of the commandments in the Pentateuch may bespeak agnostic tendencies—is supported, as a matter of intellectual history, by the related facts that, in his lifetime, Maimonides was charged by some traditionalists with at least partial adherence to the view of reality of Aristotle, and that that charge against him by traditionalists has persisted; a charge grounded in the contention that the world-view of Aristotle is, especially as considered by traditionalism, at the best, agnostic, and, at the worst, atheistic, because it contends that human beings, intelligent enough and well enough disciplined, can comprehend all of reality, and that in consequence to posit any theism—in particular, the monotheism of the Pentateuch—is to impede understanding.

Traditionalists convinced of Maimonides' reverence for the God of the Torah, for the sacred history it narrates, and for the codex it mandates, have been confident that it bespeaks, decisively and unambiguously, his traditionalism. Others, however, have suspected that that traditionalism is undermined, perhaps even nullified, by at least his suspicion, and perhaps even his conviction, that Aristotle is correct in considering *mysterium* a decisive impediment to understanding.

That both groups of traditionalists have, without resolving the matter, disagreed through more than eight centuries about the influence of Aristotle upon Maimonides indicates, in the opinion of the present study, that, at the minimum, to reject summarily the plausible conjecture noted is inappropriate; that, to the contrary, the application of intellect to understand why, in the Pentateuch, God did what He did, should be regarded by traditionalism with caution perhaps indistinguishable from wariness.

That traditionalism should so regard it is indicated less forcefully by reference to the history of ideas, which accounts only for the attitude of a class of traditionalists towards the two inseparable texts, the Written Law and the Oral Law—that is to say, towards the Torah—upon which alone traditionalism as a view of reality is grounded, than by reference to the thesis of the present study: that the Pentateuch cannot, in significant measure, perhaps even typically, be comprehended, because its view of reality is marked by, perhaps even defined by, *mysterium*.

Maimonides concedes that the laws that govern the red heifer may be inaccessible to reason. That commandment aside, as he begins, in Chapter 27, the task of rationalizing virtually all of God's other commandments he notes that, when he has finished, "only very few *commandments* will remain whose cause has not been clear to me,"[33] and ten chapters later asserts that he has failed to grasp the cause of those very few only "up to this time."[34]

The Gemara that, by contrast, Rashi references asserts that it is forbidden even to think only about *chukim*. It does not interdict thinking about the laws in the codex that are not *chukim*. But nothing in Rashi's encyclopedic work indicates that thinking about, in particular, what God was, so to speak, thinking when He mandated the codex concerned him; or whether traditionalists can access the mind, so to speak, of God, when they interpret and mandate law (or when, for that matter, they interpret sacred history). Except, perhaps, when he references the oblique domain of Midrash, nothing in his work indicates, or even hints, that Rashi imagines any human being can enter into, so to speak, the mind of God. And nothing indicates that either The Babylonian or Jerusalem Talmud is interested in such matters. By contrast, it is difficult, at the minimum, to understand why a traditionalist convinced that he understands why God mandated virtually all of the laws in the Torah would doubt his ability, or that of any traditionalist intelligent enough and well enough disciplined, to access the mind, so to speak, of God when interpreting and mandating law, or, if the matter concerned him, when interpreting sacred history.

---

33. Maimonides, *Guide*, p. 510.
34. Ibid., p. 538.

As regards the spectrum of traditionalism represented at its ends by Rashi and Maimonides, the preference that derives from the text itself upon which alone traditionalism is grounded is, in the opinion of the present study, unmistakable; as is the conviction of the study that submission to it is the indispensable precondition of understanding.

Appendix 1

The position that the Pentateuch traditionalists study today is not essentially the same Pentateuch God dictated to Moses at the Revelation on Mount Sinai is advocated in detail by Marc B. Shapiro.[1] In the opinion of the present study, that position is obviated by a survey of relevant biblical history that for traditionalists perforce corroborates a theological axiom.

Between the time God dictated the Pentateuch (the Written Law) and the Mishnah (the Oral Law)[2] to Moses[3] during the Revelation and the time the First Temple was destroyed, an uncorrupted text of the Pentateuch existed. According to Deuteronomy 31:24-26, Moses wrote it and placed it in, or near, the Ark of the Covenant[4] shortly before he died, thirty-nine years after the Revelation. From that time until the First Temple was destroyed, the uncorrupted text remained in the Holiest of Holies. During that period

---

1. *The Limits of Orthodox Theology* (Portland, OR: 2005), pp. 91-121.

2. That during the Revelation at Mount Sinai God taught Moses the Oral Law is axiomatic for traditionalists. Opinions vary, however, regarding how many of the mishnayot contained in the written text, known as the Mishnah, redacted from a text transmitted orally for centuries constitute the Oral Law. (For a minimalist opinion formulated by Maimonides, see pp. 118-121, above.)

3. As Deuteronomy 31:9 indicates, Moses wrote the Pentateuch, and assembled the Mishnah, only a short time before he died, and in the land of Moab (32:49), rather than at Mount Sinai. Nevertheless, on the authority of the Mishnah (Pirke Avot 1:1), traditionalism asserts that Moses "received the Torah at Mount Sinai," perhaps on the understanding that God dictated the Pentateuch to him during the eighty (or one hundred and twenty) days he spent with Him on Mount Sinai; and that during that time He also taught him those mishnayot that constitute the Oral Law, and that were transmitted orally until the time of the "Great Assembly," or Sanhedrin, a judicial institution that persisted into the Common Era (CE), when Rabbi Yehuda ha'Nasi compiled the Mishnah, a volume that contained both those mishnayot that constitute the Oral Law, and others.

4. Whether the scroll was placed in the Ark itself or in a container adjacent to the Ark is disputed in Bava Basra 14b. That it was in one of those places is not disputed.

Appendix 1

the Pentateuch "must have been in the Ark. Otherwise it could not have come from the destruction of Shiloh to Solomon's Temple. It was never lost; being in the Ark, in the Holiest of Holies, it was only accessible to the High Priest on Yom Kippur. It simply was not asked for all these centuries."[5] What happened to it immediately after the First Temple was destroyed is not known. Sometime between when Ezra returned to the land of Israel, and when he died, he presented the Pentateuch again to the Jewish people - the same Pentateuch that Moses had received at Mount Sinai, as the Book of Nechemiah recounts in detail (8:1-38), and as the Babylonian Talmud confirms in asserting that "it was presented to them again in the days of Ezra."[6]

From the time of Ezra to the beginning of the Common Era (CE), and for centuries thereafter, scholarly attention devoted to such Pentateuchs as appeared assessed their accuracy by comparison to Ezra's Pentateuch; until, during the tenth century, a document of the Pentateuch was redacted known as the Masoretic text, the text still accepted by traditionalists as canonical.

The biblical history above supports the conclusion that from the Revelation to about the beginning of the Common Era the Pentateuch that Moses wrote was essentially uncorrupted. That being the case, unless during three subsequent centuries (about 700–1000 CE) evidence of major discrepancies was discovered by Masoretic scholarship, it is reasonable to conclude that from the Revelation to the redaction of the Masoretic text in the tenth century CE—that is to say, through about twenty-three—the Pentateuch that Moses was taught "at Sinai" was essentially uncorrupted.

That during the three centuries of Masoretic editing no major discrepancies were discovered is affirmed even by Shapiro, who grants that "there is no question that it is not improper, to continue to refer to 'the Masoretic text,' and in the pages that follow I shall do so. The minor variations simply enforce the fact that there is an overwhelming measure of agreement."[7] And since that is the case, it is reasonable to conclude that, except as regards vocalization, the Masoretic enterprise was remarkably unproductive, because over about three centuries it edited a text that required no significant editing.

5. Heinrich W. Guggenheimer (email communication dated September 8, 2015, to the author)

6. *Talmud Bavli*, Sanhedrin, 21b. For traditionalism, that the Talmud acknowledges that the letters in Ezra's Pentateuch were different from those in Moses' Pentateuch, and nonetheless maintains that the two Pentateuchs were the same confirms that the change in letters caused no corruption in the transmission of Moses' Pentateuch.

7. *Limits*, p.92, fn. 11.

Appendix 1

That it did not require such editing is demonstrated by the survey of biblical history above. That, as a theological matter, it could not for traditionalists have required such editing is demonstrated by the brief discussion below of God's intention as regards the Revelation.

Beyond question, because He has always loved the Jewish people unfathomably, God erupted into human history at Mount Sinai to give to them alone the most precious of His gifts: a document in two parts—the Pentateuch (the Written Law) and the Mishnah (the Oral Law)—that is to say, the Torah—that alone can teach only them how to effect a transcendent aspiration: how to cling to Him in love. In that clinging alone, Deuteronomy 4:4 asserts, is life: "Only you, the ones who remained attached to God your Lord, are still alive today." And the Jewish people can achieve life only in measure as they obey the commandments stipulated, often, perhaps even for the most part, cryptically in the Written Law, and explained in minute detail in the Oral Law; and they are therefore commanded in Leviticus 18:5 to "Keep My decrees and laws, since it is only by keeping them that a person can [truly] live."

That the statement above describes God's intention is demonstrated by Deuteronomy 7:6-8,11. As Moses informs the Jewish people,

> [6] You are a nation consecrated to God your Lord. God your Lord chose you to be His special people among all the nations on the face of the earth. [7] It was not because you had greater numbers than all the other nations that God embraced you and chose you; you are among the smallest of all the nations. [8] It was because of God's love for you and because He was keeping the oath that He made to your fathers . . . [11] So safeguard the mandate, the rules and laws that I am teaching you today, so that you will keep them.

Because the statement above describes pellucidly God's intention as regards the Revelation at Mount Sinai, that He would not permit the document—the Torah—His sole guide to its implementation to become corrupted is axiomantic. That is to say, as the present study shows, both the Pentateuch and the Mishnah often, perhaps even typically, confound intellection by underscoring mysterium. But mysterium and corruption are different matters. A God who loves his people profoundly may, for reasons that cannot be known, promote incomprehension. But that He would not permit corruption to infect the document indispensable to the transcendent aspiration of His chosen people is self-evident.

Appendix 1

In the opinion of the present study, the essential proof that the Torah Moses received at Mount Sinai is essentially the Torah redacted about twenty-three centuries later is contained in the theological statement above. The relevant biblical history merely corroborates the statement, because for traditionalists it must. That is to say, the Torah has passed uncorrupted through history from the Revelation at Mount Sinai to the present day, and will continue to pass uncorrupted through history until history ends, because God intends that it should, and therefore it must. To secular scholarship that is obscurantism. To traditionalism it is faith.

Bibliography

The Babylonian Talmud. Edited by Isidor Epstein, 30 volumes. London: Soncino:1936-83.
The Chumash [the Pentateuch]. Translated by Nosson Sherman. New York: Mesorah, 2002.
Guggenheimer, Heinrich W. *Jerusalem Talmud: Ta'aniot, Megillah, Hagigah, Mo'ed Qatan.* Berlin: DeGruyter, 2015.
The Living Torah [the Pentateuch]. Translated by Aryeh Kaplan. New York: Moznaim, 1981.
Maimonides, Moses. *The Guide of the Perplexed.* Translated by Shlomo Pines. 2 volumes. Chicago University Press, 1963.
———. *Moses Maimonides' Commentary on The Mishnah.* Translated by Fred Rosner. New York: Feldheim, 1975.
———. *Mishneh Torah, Hilchot De'ot & Hilchot Talmud Torah.* Translated by Ze'ev Abramson & Eliyahu Touger. New York: Moznaim, 1989.
———. *Mishneh Torah, Hilchot Tefillah II.* Translated by Eliyahu Touger. 2 volumes. New York: Moznaim, 1989.
———. *Mishneh Torah, Sefer Ha'avodah.* Translated by Eliyahu Touger. New York: Moznaim, 2009.
———. *Mishneh Torah, Sefer Hakorbanot.* Translated by Eliyahu Touger. New York: Moznaim, 2007.
Nachshoni, Yehuda. *Studies in the Weekly Parshah.* Translated by Shmuel Himmelstein, et al. 5 volumes. New York: Mesorah, 1989.
Sefer Hachinuch. Translated by Charles Wengrow. 5 volumes. New York: Feldheim, 2012.
Shapiro, Marc B. *The Limits of Orthodox Theology.* Oxford: Littman, 2005.
Soloveitchik, Joseph B. *The Halahic Mind.* New York: Macmillan, 1986.
Talmud Bavli [The Babylonian Talmud]. Edited by Yisroel Simcha Schorr. 72 volumes. New York: Mesorah, 1990-2005.

www.ingramcontent.com/pod-product-compliance
Lightning Source LLC
Chambersburg PA
CBHW071508150426
43191CB00009B/1450